I'M A RAMBLER
I'M A GAMBLER
I'M A LONG WAY FROM HOME
AND IF YOU DON'T LIKE ME
WELL, LEAVE ME ALONE
I EAT WHEN I'M HUNGRY
I DRINK WHEN I'M DRY
AND THE MOONSHINE DON'T KILL ME
I'LL LIVE 'TILL I DIE

From "The Moonshiner," an Irish folk song

home made
winter

yvette van boven

photography
oof verschuren

STEWART, TABORI & CHANG
NEW YORK

handy:

* ALL RECIPES SERVE 4, UNLESS OTHERWISE INDICATED.

* 1 TBSP = 15 G   * 1 TSP = 5 G

* BAKING TIMES MAY BE LONGER OR SHORTER IN DIFFERENT OVENS. THE BAKING TIMES IN THIS BOOK ARE THEREFORE SUGGESTIONS. PLEASE RELY ON YOUR EXPERIENCE WITH YOUR OWN OVEN.

* I OFTEN USE CAGE-FREE EGGS (LARGE), BUT I MUCH PREFER USING FREE-RANGE OR ORGANIC EGGS.

* 1 LITER = 10 DL = 100 CL = 1000 ML

* ALWAYS USE FREE-RANGE OR, EVEN BETTER, ORGANIC MEAT. AND THIS IS MANDATORY!

⅓ CRANBERRY JUICE
⅓ GINGER ALE
⅓ VODKA

WELCOME COCKTAIL!

YES! → THAT'S ME INDEED!.
PHOTOGRAPHED BY OOF (110 YEARS AGO)

PUBLISHED IN 2012
BY STEWART, TABORI & CHANG, AN IMPRINT OF ABRAMS

text, food styling, prop styling, design & illustrations:
YVETTE VAN BOVEN

photography: OOF VERSCHUREN
RENSKE KUIPER P. 69, TOP RIGHT
MARIETTE & VICTOR VAN BOVEN, PP. 43 & 193

~~edcting, editen, editxng:~~ HENNIE FRANSSEN-SEEBREGTS

FOR ABRAMS
EDITOR: NATALIE KAIRE
DESIGNER: LIAM FLANAGAN
TRANSLATOR: MARLEEN REIMER
PRODUCTION MANAGER: ANET SIRNA-BRUDER

CATALOGING-IN-PUBLICATION DATA HAS BEEN APPLIED FOR AND MAY BE OBTAINED FROM THE LIBRARY OF CONGRESS.

ISBN 978-1-61769-004-4

©2012 YVETTE VAN BOVEN

ORIGINALLY PUBLISHED IN 2011 BY FONTAINE UITGEVERS

STEWART, TABORI & CHANG BOOKS ARE AVAILABLE AT SPECIAL DISCOUNTS WHEN PURCHASED IN QUANTITY FOR PREMIUMS AND PROMOTIONS AS WELL AS FUNDRAISING OR EDUCATIONAL USE. SPECIAL EDITIONS CAN ALSO BE CREATED TO SPECIFICATION. FOR DETAILS, CONTACT SPECIALSALES@ABRAMSBOOKS.COM OR THE ADDRESS BELOW.

ABRAMS
THE ART OF BOOKS SINCE 1949
115 WEST 18TH STREET
NEW YORK, NY 10011
WWW.ABRAMSBOOKS.COM

introduction

When I finished writing *Home Made*, I realized I actually wasn't quite done. There were still heaps of recipes, waiting wistfully, and every day new ones were added. So it was tough to say good-bye.

But oh well—at some point you need to let the book go because the printer is waiting for it and because people are waiting for the book in the bookstore. I went with the book to the printer in Spain, then I went with the book to the bookstore, and occasionally I would accompany the book to its future home and write a farewell note in it.

That's all I could do. Making such a big book is a real undertaking. I lived with the book and it stayed with me day and night. So once it was finished and had left my home, I began to miss it tremendously. I missed thinking about the contents of the book, I missed writing, drawing, continuously looking to see if there'd be something even more delightful to add, killing off some of my dearest darling recipes, finding more that I'd been looking for forever, traveling to unfamiliar destinations to photograph them with my husband, Oof, and going on new adventures. I missed photographing the dishes, eating them together, and gleefully realizing that each was another truly fun recipe.

In the meantime, more recipes and ideas were piling up high and my fingers were itching to get started again. I talked about the missing and the itching with my publisher. Luckily, he agreed that I should develop my plans into a new book. No, wait: not one new book; it would have to be two. One turned out to be insufficient for all I wanted to tell, so after this one, there will be another.

Because I grew up in a pretty wet and cold country (Ireland), and now spend a lot of time in a warmer one (France), I've rendered that into two volumes: Winter and Summer. In this first volume, Winter, you'll find more Irish meals, and in the Summer book, more French meals.

Because I'm often headstrong, I've sometimes interpreted things completely my own way, and I hope you won't mind. Because I'm often impatient, I've sometimes drawn the recipes because it's faster than writing. And because at times, probably unnecessarily, I worry that you won't understand quite what I'm trying to say, I've also added memories and photos so you get a sense of what I mean. I believe that, just like a formally decorated table or a beautifully arranged plate, a cookbook should exude a certain spirit, or a mood, that you should be in when you start to get going in the kitchen. My first book has packed her suitcase and is embarking on a trip around the world, and I'll go with her. I'm working on a new cookbook now, and I'll see you soon, when the sun is shining and we can eat outdoors. Something delicious. But in the meantime, cook the winter away. It's going to be a good one.

Yvette

Wicklow Mountains, Ireland

Co. Kerry, Ireland

contents

Les Acc

Beignets créo

(Morue, Poulet, Toma

BREAKFAST
BRUNCH
LUNCH

bannock bread

You can make this bread in no time, and you cook it in a pan so you don't need an oven! It will become a sort of thick pancake, which you'll cut into wedges. The taste and texture are similar to those of scones. Serve with salted butter, clotted cream, or unsweetened whipped cream, and fresh strawberries or jams. You can make my "Devonshire" cream (recipe below) instead of buying clotted cream, which is not always easy to find.

2 cups (250 g) all-purpose flour
2 tbsp sugar
½ tsp baking powder
½ tsp baking soda
½ tsp salt
3 tbsp (40 g) butter, plus more for
    the pan
about 1 cup (225 ml) buttermilk

Combine the dry ingredients in a bowl. Cut in the butter until the mixture resembles a coarse meal, then quickly stir in the buttermilk until the dough is nicely smooth and compact. Don't knead too long or the bread will become tough. It should be crumbly, much like a scone.

Pat it into a flat round loaf that will fit in a medium-size skillet.

Melt some butter in the skillet over high heat. Let the pan become very hot, then place the dough in the pan. After about 6–7 minutes, when the bottom starts to turn golden brown, you can gently turn the bread and cook it for another 7 minutes on the other side.

Let the bread cool slightly on a paper towel and cut it into wedges to serve.

my "devonshire" cream

¾ cup (200 ml) heavy cream
⅔ cup (150 g) mascarpone
seeds from 1 vanilla bean
1 tbsp superfine sugar
1 tbsp grated lemon or lime zest

With a hand mixer, beat all the ingredients into a fluffy cream. Leave to stiffen in the fridge.

Eat with wedges of bannock bread and raspberry jam or quince jam with star anise & cardamom (recipe below).

QUINCE JAM WITH STAR ANISE & CARDAMOM
FOR ABOUT 4 JARS

IN A FOOD PROCESSOR, GRATE A GENEROUS 2¼ LB (1KG) QUINCES
→ PEELED & CORED

BEWARE! THEY'RE TOUGH!

↳ WATCH YOUR FINGERS!

BRING THE QUINCES TO A BOIL WITH 4½ CUPS (1L) WATER & 5 CUPS (1KG) SUGAR & THE JUICE OF 1 LEMON. ADD 3 STAR ANISE & 8 CARDAMOM PODS. BOIL DOWN ON LOW HEAT FOR ABOUT AN HOUR. SPOON INTO CLEAN JARS.
→ REFRIGERATE ←

cardamom & orange scones

FOR ABOUT 12 SCONES

4 cups (500 g) self-rising flour
3 tbsp superfine sugar
pinch of salt
3 tbsp (40 g) butter
1 cup (250 ml) milk
3 tbsp (65 g) marmalade
1 tsp freshly ground cardamom
    seeds

FOR THE GLAZE
¼ cup (85 g) marmalade
1 tsp freshly ground cardamom
    seeds
grated zest of 1 orange

FOR THE MASCARPONE CREAM
1 tbsp orange blossom water
1 tbsp honey
1 cup plus 1 tbsp (250 g)
    mascarpone

Make the scones: Sift the flour, sugar, and salt into a bowl. Cut the butter into small chunks and add it to the flour mixture; use a fork to work the mixture into a crumbly dough. Add the milk, marmalade, and cardamom. Work the mixture quickly and lightly into a smooth dough. Don't knead too long or the scones will be tough.

On a lightly floured surface, roll out the dough to ¾-inch (2-cm) thick. With a biscuit cutter or drinking glass, cut 2½-inch (6-cm) rounds. Place them on a baking sheet lined with parchment paper. Reroll the scraps and cut more rounds.

Let the scones stand for 15 minutes before baking, or make them the night before and let them rest in a cool spot.

Preheat the oven to 450°F (240°C). That's hot!

Bake the scones for 12 to 15 minutes, until golden brown.

Make the glaze: In a saucepan, heat the marmalade with 2 tbsp water, stir in the cardamom, then press the mixture through a sieve into a bowl.

Brush the scones with the glaze and sprinkle them with the orange zest.

Make the cream: Fold the orange blossom water and honey into the mascarpone and whip until airy.

Serve the scones with the mascarpone cream.

GINGERBREAD

— OR PAIN D'EPICE —
(IT SOUNDS A LOT FANCIER
IN FRENCH)

GREASE A
4-BY-8 INCH
LOAF PAN
(1 LITER)
WITH SOFT
BUTTER

PREHEAT THE
OVEN TO 300°F
(150 °C / GAS 2)

MIX +

POUR THE
BATTER INTO
THE PAN. BAKE
THE CAKE 1 HR
UNTIL GOLDEN

3¼ CUPS (400 G) SELF-RISING FLOUR

A PINCH OF SALT
1 TEASPOON OF EACH:
→ GROUND GINGER
→ GROUND CINNAMON
→ GROUND CORIANDER
& A PINCH OF GROUND ALLSPICE

½ CUP (100 G) PACKED LIGHT BROWN SUGAR
¼ CUP + 3 TBS (150 G) HONEY
¾ CUP + 1 TBS (200 ML) MILK

↠ LET IT COOL ON A RACK AND THEN WRAP IT ↞
SO IT'LL STAY NICE & MOIST

orange snowman shake

FOR 4 SERVINGS

1⅔ cups (400 ml) orange juice
¾ cup (200 ml) milk
1⅔ cups (400 ml) vanilla ice cream
seeds from 1 vanilla bean
1 tsp ground ginger

Mix all the ingredients in a blender until foamy. Pour immediately into tall glasses.

neil's zingy juice cocktail

During one of our trips to southwest Ireland, we stayed in a bed and breakfast where we were so welcomingly received that it almost frightened us. They prepared everything for breakfast themselves, including this wonderful cocktail. Perfect host Neil gave me the recipe as soon as I asked.

FOR 2 SERVINGS

¾ cup (200 ml) fresh orange juice
¾ cup (200 ml) cranberry juice
¾ inch (2 cm) peeled fresh ginger,
    grated

Mix all the ingredients in a blender until foamy. Let it rest (15 minutes works, but 1 hour is better), then strain through a sieve and serve.

banana smoothie

FOR 4 SERVINGS

2 cups (500 ml) plain yogurt
2 bananas
1 cup (250 ml) orange or
    clementine juice
1 tbsp honey
pinch of freshly grated nutmeg

Mix the yogurt, bananas, orange or clementine juice, and honey in a blender until foamy. Pour immediately into tall glasses. Garnish with the nutmeg.

winter tea

I nurse a pathetic addiction to zoethoutthee, *licorice root tea. First I bought it in teabags in an organic store, until I found out that the chic tea store sold it as loose tea, which was even more delicious! And then I thought: "I can of course also make it myself. Licorice root—you can buy that in every drugstore." You'll need to boil the tea a relatively long time because you'll be using an entire stick. But if you keep adding water, one batch of ingredients will last all day. That's what I do.*

FOR 6 SERVINGS

3 slices fresh ginger
1 stick of licorice root
1 cinnamon stick
1 tsp grated orange zest
1 clove

Put the ginger and licorice root in a saucepan, add 4½ cups (1 l) water, and bring to a boil. Lower the heat and let it simmer for 5 minutes. Take the pan off the heat and add all the remaining ingredients.

Let the tea steep for another 15 minutes.

Strain through a sieve into a teapot or mugs.

butter

Maybe it's me, but I find homemade butter much tastier than butter from a store. It's just . . . creamier. It could also be that I find it tastier because I've made it myself. Oh, whatever. It's good! And fun and quick to make.

You know what's also good? To mix it with flaky Maldon sea salt or very fine salt and little lavender flowers. Spread it thickly on warm toast and eat with a soft-boiled egg.

1. **beat** 4½ cups (1 l) cream for a long time, with a mixer, until it looks like scrambled eggs. **2. pour** the cream into a clean dish towel that you've placed over a strainer. Collect the whey (the liquid) in a bowl; you can use it to make soda bread (page 23). Wring the butter as much as possible. **3. knead** it in a bowl of ice water, changing the water 2 or 3 times, until the water remains clear. This step is important because if there's any whey left, the butter can quickly turn rancid. **4. soak** two wooden spatulas in another bowl of cold water. Use them to shape the butter into a nice bar. Wrap your butter in parchment paper and store in the fridge. It will remain fresh for at least 2 weeks! This recipe will yield about ¾ cup (300 g) butter.

crackle butter

The name may be a bit childish, but I call it this because the salt crystals crackle so nicely when you chew on them.

½ cup plus 2 tbsp (150 g) butter
2 tbsp flaky sea salt, such as Maldon

anchovy butter

Mmm, nice on a warm baguette, just plain, or with tomatoes.

1 cup plus 2 tbsp (250 g) butter
1 tin anchovy fillets, drained and mashed
1 tbsp fresh lemon juice
1 tbsp minced fresh parsley

horseradish butter

Good with ham, cured meat, or sausage.

½ cup plus 2 tbsp (150 g) butter
2 tbsp prepared horseradish, or 1 tbsp very finely grated
    fresh horseradish
2 tbsp minced fresh chives
pinch of salt

ginger lime butter

Melt a bit on a pan-seared fish fillet.

½ cup plus 2 tbsp (150 g) butter
1 thumb-size piece fresh ginger, peeled and grated
1 tbsp grated lime zest
1 tbsp fresh lime juice
pinch of salt
coarsely ground black pepper

flower butter

It may sound old-fashioned, but try it on toast with a soft-boiled egg and you'll realize that old-fashioned can be good.

½ cup plus 2 tbsp (150 g) butter
2 tbsp dried lavender, violets, or other edible flowers
    (available in organic markets), crushed
1 tbsp flaky sea salt, such as Maldon

chocolate butter

Suddenly I remembered that my mother used to make this. I tried it out at once—delicious!

½ cup plus 2 tbsp (150 g) butter
2 generous tbsp unsweetened cocoa powder
pinch of salt
seeds from 1 vanilla bean
3 tbsp confectioners' sugar

almond lemon butter

7 tbsp (100 g) butter
⅔ cup (100 g) whole almonds, lightly toasted and
    coarsely ground
1 tbsp grated lemon zest
1 tsp honey

cinnamon butter

I don't have anything to add to this . . .

½ cup plus 2 tbsp (150 g) butter
3 tbsp plus 1 tsp (75 g) honey
1 tbsp cinnamon
pinch of salt
3 tbsp ground walnuts or pecans

seeded butter

½ cup plus 2 tbsp (150 g) butter

Briefly toast and coarsely grind before mixing:
2 tbsp caraway seed
2 tbsp cumin seed
1 tbsp coriander seed
1 tbsp coarse sea salt

In our restaurant, we mix the butter at room temperature and roll it in plastic wrap to firm up in the fridge. Then we precut the slices and keep them in a bowl of ice water until we need them, so they don't stick together. You could use this method for slicing, or simply pack the butter in ramekins covered with plastic wrap. >>>

brown soda bread

In my previous book, Home Made, *I gave you a simple recipe for soda bread, the bread my mother used to make for us. The recipe below I ferreted out myself because I love a bit more texture in my bread. Whenever I buy soda bread in Ireland nowadays, it often has this nice texture—see, that's what I wanted to make at home! Here's the recipe! > Oh yeah: Eat this with your homemade butter and, instead of the buttermilk in the recipe, use the whey that you collected when you made the butter. Everything* Home Made, *of course, honestly authentic.*

4 cups (500 g) whole wheat flour
2½ cups (200 g) rolled oats
1⅔ cups (100 g) wheat bran
3 generous tbsp brown sugar
pinch of salt
1 tsp baking soda
2 cups (500 ml) buttermilk or whey,
    or more or less as needed to
    make a smooth dough
1 egg, beaten

Preheat the oven to 350°F (180°C).

Combine the dry ingredients in a large bowl. Add the buttermilk and egg and stir until the dough just comes together in a ball—no longer, or the bread will be tough.

Grease a 9-inch (23-cm) round cake pan and pat the dough into it. Brush the top with some water and sprinkle with some bran or oats, then slash a cross into the top. Bake for about 45 minutes. Take the bread out of the pan and bake directly on the oven rack for another 10 minutes, until it is nicely browned and crisp. Let it cool on a rack.

irish whiskey soda bread

For the traditionalists!

1 cup (150 g) mixed raisins and
    currants
1½ tsp caraway seed
4 tbsp Irish whiskey
8 cups (1 kg) all-purpose flour
3 tbsp sugar
1 tbsp baking powder
½ tsp baking soda
pinch of salt
¼ cup (50 g) butter, at room
    temperature
2 eggs
1⅔ cups (400 ml) buttermilk, or
    more or less as needed to make a
    smooth dough

Preheat the oven to 400°F (200°C).

Mix the raisins and currants with the caraway seeds and whiskey and let soak for about 15 minutes. In a large bowl, combine the flour, sugar, baking powder, baking soda, and salt, then work in the butter until the mixture resembles a coarse meal.

Spoon the raisin-whiskey mixture quickly through the flour mixture. Beat the eggs. Reserve 2 spoonfuls of egg in a small bowl and add the rest to the buttermilk. Pour that over the flour mixture and knead until it just comes together in a ball—no longer!

Form a smooth ball of dough, lift it onto a baking sheet, and brush it with the leftover egg. With a sharp knife, carve a small cross in the middle.

Bake for 40 to 45 minutes, until the bread sounds hollow when you tap on the bottom. Let it cool on a rack.

farls with smoked trout, capers, lemon & parsley

These Irish farls resemble blinis, but they are made of boiled potatoes instead of buckwheat flour. You can easily prepare the dough and cream cheese topping the night before, so that you'll only need to fry the farls in the morning. Perfect for brunch. Instead of trout you can, of course, use any smoked fish, or even smoked meat.

FOR THE FARLS
3 potatoes in their skins
¾ cup (100 g) self-rising flour
pinch of salt

ON TOP
½ small red onion, diced
2 tbsp finely chopped fresh parsley
grated zest of 1 lemon
2 tbsp drained capers
6 oz (150 g) cream cheese

AND FURTHER
3 tbsp (50 g) butter, for frying
7 oz (200 g) smoked fish: trout,
    halibut, or salmon

Boil the potatoes until tender, peel them, then pass them through a potato ricer (or mash with a potato masher). Mix with the self-rising flour and salt and swiftly knead into a smooth dough. Roll into a sausage shape about 2½ inches (6 cm) thick and wrap in plastic wrap. Place in the refrigerator until ready to use, up to overnight.

In a food processor, process the onion, parsley, lemon zest, and capers until finely minced. Take one half out of the bowl and keep covered in the fridge until ready to use. Add the cream cheese to the other half and pulse briefly to combine. Cover the cream cheese mixture and store it in the fridge. You can do all of this a day in advance.

Unwrap the roll of dough and cut it into ¼-inch (6-mm) thick slices. They are a little sticky but you can handle them easily with a pancake spatula rinsed in cold water.

Heat a little butter in a nonstick skillet. Fry the farls quickly on both sides until golden brown.

Serve 2 or 3 per person. Cover with a generous portion of smoked fish. Serve with the cream cheese mixture and sprinkle with the minced herb mixture.

oatmeal & fruit scones

These are light, sweet, crumbly scones that are ready in no time. Serve with unsweetened crème fraîche and grapefruit & lime curd (facing page).

2½ cups (300 g) self-rising flour
2½ cups (200 g) rolled oats
2 tbsp confectioners' sugar
2 tsp baking powder
3½ oz (100 g) chopped dried apple
    and pear
pinch of salt
grated zest of 1 orange
½ cup plus 2 tbsp (150 g) butter, at
    room temperature
¾ cup (200 ml) buttermilk,
    or more as needed to make a
    smooth dough
1 egg, beaten

Preheat the oven to 400°F (200°C).

Combine all the dry ingredients in a large bowl. Quickly blend in the butter and buttermilk to form a smooth dough without overmixing. On a lightly floured surface, pat the dough out into an even slab. With a cutter or drinking glass, cut 2½-inch (6 cm) scones. Place on a baking sheet lined with parchment paper and brush each scone with egg.

Bake for about 12-15 minutes, until light golden brown.

On our way to Sally Gap, Wicklow, Ireland

GRAPEFRUIT & LIME CURD

BEAT WITH A HAND MIXER:

2 EGGS + 2 EGG YOLKS
½ CUP + 2 TBSP (125G) SUGAR
& ½ CUP (125 ML) GRAPEFRUIT +
LIME JUICE

← LOOK : DO THIS "AU BAIN MARIE"
IN A BOWL ON TOP OF A PAN
OF GENTLY BOILING WATER.
MAKE SURE THAT THE BOWL DOESN'T
TOUCH THE WATER, THOUGH.

⟹ BEAT UNTIL THE MIXTURE IS AS THICK AS YOGURT ⟸

TAKE THE BOWL
OFF THE HEAT,
THEN WHISK IN
5 TBSP (75G)
COLD BUTTER
IN SMALL CHUNKS

LET IT COOL
COMPLETELY,
THEN PUT
IN THE
FRIDGE
UNTIL IT'S
REALLY COLD.

yogurt

In France almost everybody owns a yaourtière: a yogurt maker. When I wanted to buy one just after Christmas, they were sold out everywhere. It can't be that difficult, I thought, because the only thing that machine does is keep your mixture at a steady temperature. Nothing my oven can't do. There's really nothing to it. The first time you make it, you'll need some yogurt from the store. Pick an organic yogurt—the fresher the better because that will contain the most active yogurt cultures. From then on, you'll want to keep a small jar of homemade yogurt aside for the next batch.

You can eat homemade yogurt every day. And feel free to add flavorings to your own taste. Experiment!

FOR ABOUT 5 CUPS (1.2 l) **1.** ʜᴇᴀᴛ 4½ cups (1 l) milk (this may be cow or goat milk) to exactly 100°F (40°C), then add ¾ cup plus 1 tbsp (200 ml) of the freshest organic yogurt. **2.** ᴘᴏᴜʀ this mixture into small clean jars. You can also first season the milk mixture with something tasty (such as honey) or first fill the jars with something (such as chopped figs). Remember to save 1 jar of plain yogurt for the next batch. **3.** ᴘʟᴀᴄᴇ all the jars, uncovered, on a baking sheet and place it in the oven, preheated to 100°F (40°C). Let them sit there for 6 hours, without opening the oven. I do this before I go to bed. **4.** ʀᴇᴍᴏᴠᴇ the jars from the oven, put the lids on, and place them in the fridge to thicken and cool completely. Store for about 1 week.

ginger yogurt with citrus salad

FOR THE SALAD

2 pink or white grapefruit

3 clementines

2 navel or blood oranges

2 tbsp ginger syrup from a jar of
    preserved ginger

½ tsp cinnamon

¼ cup pomegranate seeds

fresh mint leaves, coarsely chopped

FOR THE YOGURT

2 cups (500 ml) homemade yogurt
    (page 28)

1 cup (150 g) chopped preserved
    ginger

2 tbsp brown sugar

Make the salad: Place the grapefruit on a cutting board. With a sharp knife, slice off the top and bottom of the fruit to reveal the flesh. Slice down the sides of the fruit all the way around, cutting off enough peel and pith that you reveal the flesh. Above a bowl, cut out the flesh segments between the membranes, and collect the juice in the same bowl. Repeat for the clementines and oranges. Add the ginger syrup, cinnamon, and pomegranate seeds, cover the bowl, and set aside in the refrigerator until ready to use. You can do this the night before.

Make the yogurt: Combine the yogurt, preserved ginger, and brown sugar in a bowl. Whisk until the sugar dissolves. Put the yogurt in the fridge to allow the flavors to develop. You can do this the day before as well.

Just before serving: Mix the mint leaves with the salad. Divide the yogurt among 4 nice coupes and spoon the salad on top, leaving most of the juice behind.

chocolate yogurt

When I was little, we had chocolate yogurt from Yoplait in Ireland. It came in little conic containers, and I believe it was even topped with a layer of lemon. I've never forgotten that taste; I thought it was the best thing ever. I haven't come across that yogurt in a long time, so I decided to make it myself. I experimented a little, until the taste came close to what I remembered. Here is the recipe.

4½ cups (1 l) whole milk

¾ cup plus 1 tbsp (200 ml) organic
    yogurt

5 tbsp unsweetened cocoa powder

1½ tsp vanilla extract

3 tbsp confectioners' sugar

Preheat the oven to 100°F (40°C).

Put the milk in a saucepan and heat to 100°F (40°C).

Carefully stir in the yogurt, cocoa powder, vanilla, and confectioners' sugar. Pour the mixture into clean, small jars; place them, uncovered, on a baking sheet, and place the baking sheet in the oven for 6 hours.

Remove the baking sheet from the oven, put the lids on the jars, and place them in the refrigerator to cool and thicken.

fig & orange blossom yogurt

4½ cups (1 l) whole milk

6 fresh or dried figs

¾ cup plus 1 tbsp (200 ml) organic
    yogurt

1 tbsp orange blossom water

2 tbsp confectioners' sugar
    (optional)

Preheat the oven to 100°F (40°C).

Put the milk in a saucepan and heat to 100°F (40°C).

Cut the figs into small chunks and divide them among clean, small jars. Stir the yogurt and orange blossom water into the warm milk, and add the confectioners' sugar, if desired. Pour the mixture into the jars; place the jars, uncovered, on a baking sheet, and place the baking sheet in the oven for 6 hours.

Remove the baking sheet from the oven, put the lids on the jars, and place them in the refrigerator to cool and thicken.

Wicklow Mountains, Ireland

a winter "salade de chèvre chaud" with boudin noir

"How can I combine everything I love into one salad?" I thought. Well, as it turns out, that's easy.

FOR THE SALAD

10½ oz (300 g) blood sausage, such as the famous Irish Clonakilty black pudding

butter, for the pan

9 oz (250 g) wild mushrooms, such as chanterelles, shiitakes, or pieds bleus, cleaned and chopped

7 oz (200 g) mustard lettuce (or any other peppery salad greens, such as arugula, watercress, or even spinach)

2 heads Belgian endive

7 oz (200 g) soft goat cheese

FOR THE DRESSING

1 tbsp prepared mustard

1 tbsp ginger syrup from a jar of preserved ginger

4 tbsp raspberry vinegar

½ cup plus 2 tbsp (150 ml) olive oil

salt and freshly ground black pepper

1 container of purple cress or other tender edible leaves or flowers (optional)

Cut the sausage into slices. In a nonstick skillet, melt a small amount of butter over medium heat and briefly fry the slices on both sides until crisp and browned. Let them drain on a paper towel.

Preheat the broiler.

Add some butter to the skillet if necessary, and sauté the mushrooms over medium heat just to al dente, before they turn soft.

Wash the lettuce, dry it, and arrange it over 4 plates.

Cut the ends from the endive and remove the outer leaves. Separate the endive leaves and arrange them neatly among the mustard leaves.

Put the sausage on a small baking sheet. Sprinkle chunks of goat cheese on top of each sausage slice and place the baking sheet under the broiler until the cheese is golden brown.

Meanwhile, make the dressing: Whisk the mustard with the ginger syrup and vinegar. Slowly whisk in the oil and season the dressing with salt and pepper.

Arrange the grilled sausage slices and the mushrooms over the salad greens. Drizzle the dressing over the salads.

Cut the cress and sprinkle it over the salads to finish, if desired.

rarebits with pear & blue cheese

I happily eat this for breakfast. If you find it too intense for early morning, make it for a fantastic lunch with a peppery arugula or watercress salad. If you use small pieces of toast, you could serve these rarebits as an hors d'oeuvre.

10 oz (300 g) blue cheese, such as
    Stilton or Cashel blue, crumbled
5 oz (150 g) Parmesan cheese, grated
2 tbsp crème fraîche
2 eggs, beaten
2 tsp grainy prepared mustard
freshly ground black pepper
about 8 slices sourdough bread or
    German rye bread (Oberlander)
2 pears, peeled, cored, and sliced

In a bowl, mix the cheeses with the crème fraîche, eggs, and mustard. Season with pepper. Cover and refrigerate for 1 hour or overnight.

Toast the bread in a toaster until light brown.

Preheat the broiler.

Arrange the pear slices on the toast, then generously spoon the cheese mixture on top. Arrange the rarebits on a baking sheet.

Broil for 3 to 5 minutes, until they are golden brown and bubbly.

Serve with red onion & pomegranate compote (page 157) or with apple & tomato chutney (below).

apple & tomato chutney

A grown-up, chunkier version of ketchup.

Due to its tartness, this chutney goes well with foods that are a little rich: croque monsieur or rarebit (above), for example, and my imagination is also running wild with thoughts of serving it with the pulled pork on page 142.

THIS RECIPE WILL MAKE
4 LARGE JARS, FOR A TOTAL OF
4½ CUPS (1 l).

2¼ lb (1 kg) tart apples, peeled,
    cored, and diced
2¼ lb (1 kg) tomatoes, cut into
    wedges (you can peel them in
    advance but you don't have to)
2 large onions, diced
1 clove garlic, minced
½ cup (75 g) golden raisins
¾ cup (150 g) packed light brown
    sugar
1 tbsp mustard seed
1 tbsp curry powder
pinch of cayenne
pinch of freshly grated nutmeg
1 tsp ground allspice
2 tsp salt
2½ cups (600 ml) cider vinegar

Place the apples and 2¼ cups (½ l) water in a large saucepan. Bring to a boil, lower the heat, and simmer the apples, stirring occasionally, for 25 to 30 minutes, or until they're soft. Add more water if necessary—you don't want it to be dry!

Add all the remaining ingredients. Stir until the sugar is dissolved, then bring to a boil.

Turn the heat to very low and let the chutney simmer for 3 hours, stirring occasionally, until it's nice and thick.

Taste for salt and cayenne and add more if needed.

Spoon the boiling chutney into hot sterilized jars. Seal the jars with clean, new two-piece lids and turn them upside down to cool completely. The chutney will improve if you wait a month before opening it. Once opened, keep the chutney in the refrigerator.

speckled salad with quinoa, leek, bacon & chervil

FOR THE SALAD
6 baby leeks
2 tbsp olive oil
about ½ cup (150 ml) dry white
   vermouth or dry white wine
salt
⅔ cup (100 g) quinoa, well rinsed
5 oz (150 g) thinly sliced bacon
2 to 3 tbsp poppy seeds
1 bunch fresh chervil
2 handfuls baby spinach or arugula

FOR THE DRESSING
juice of 1 lemon
1 clove garlic, minced
pinch of cayenne
⅓ cup (75 ml) extra-virgin olive oil
⅓ cup (75 ml) grapeseed oil or other
   light oil
salt and freshly ground black pepper

Make the salad: Cut the leeks diagonally into ½-inch (1.5-cm) pieces. Rinse them thoroughly, drain well, then fry them in the oil in a saute pan or wok over high heat until they are really hot, but not yet browned, stirring constantly.

Add the vermouth and lower the heat. Put the lid on slightly askew and braise about 20 minutes, stirring occasionally, until the leeks are tender.

Meanwhile, bring a small saucepan of water to a boil, add a pinch of salt, and stir in the quinoa. Set a kitchen timer for 10 minutes. Let the quinoa cook gently on low heat. When the alarm goes off, immediately drain the quinoa and rinse it with cold water to halt further cooking. Let it drain thoroughly.

In a nonstick skillet, fry the bacon until crisp and let it drain on a paper towel.

The pan with the leeks should be almost dry and the leeks just about done. Lift the leeks onto a plate and let them cool. In a medium bowl, combine the leeks with the quinoa, poppy seeds, and some of the chervil. Set some chervil aside for garnish.

Make the dressing: Whisk together the lemon juice, garlic, and cayenne, then whisk in the oils in a thin stream. Season with salt and pepper. Pour over the speckled leek mixture.

Arrange the spinach in a big bowl. Add the speckled salad and crumble the bacon on top. Garnish with the reserved chervil and serve.

a somewhat arabian salad with barley and marinated mushrooms

A coarse-grained, wintry tabbouleh—and the dressing is really nice too. You could replace the barley with farro or spelt, some coarse bulgur, or wild rice.

¼ cup (50 g) barley
salt

FOR THE DRESSING
juice of 1 lemon
2 cloves garlic, minced
1½ tsp prepared hot mustard
1 tbsp *ras al hanout* (a strongly
    flavored mix of spices, including
    cinnamon, nutmeg, cardamom,
    coriander, cumin, fennel seeds,
    and others)
1 tsp salt
freshly ground black pepper
½ cup (125 ml) light vegetable oil

FOR THE SALAD
9 oz (250 g) mushrooms, cut into
    halves or quarters
9 oz (250 g) haricots verts, cut in half
1 large carrot, sliced
⅔ cup (150 g) cooked chickpeas,
    from a can if necessary, rinsed
¼ cup (20 g) chopped fresh parsley
½ cup (60 g) pecan halves, briefly
    toasted in a dry skillet

Make the barley and dressing: Rinse the barley thoroughly in a sieve. Place it in a saucepan in 3 inches (8 cm) of salted water, with the lid askew, and simmer about 40 minutes, until tender. Make sure it doesn't simmer dry.

While you cook the barley, whisk all the dressing ingredients except the oil in a large bowl. Then slowly trickle in the oil, whisking the dressing to blend it nicely.

Make the salad: Add the mushrooms to the dressing and let them marinate until ready to serve.

Blanch the haricots verts and the carrot slices separately in a saucepan of boiling salted water for a few minutes until they're al dente. Drain and rinse under cold water. Set the beans aside. Add the carrots and the chickpeas to the mushrooms in the bowl.

When the barley is done, drain it in a sieve and rinse it under cold running water. Add the barley to the vegetables in the bowl; mix well.

Sprinkle the salad with the parsley and let it sit for a least 30 minutes before serving. This will allow the various flavors to be absorbed.

Just before serving, gently fold the haricots verts and the pecans into the salad.

Bastille & Gare d' Austerliz, Paris, France

HALLOWEEN

OCTOBER 31 IS HALLOWEEN.
I USED TO BE SCARED OF WITCHES AND GHOSTS
BECAUSE IN IRELAND THEY ARE REAL, BUT ON
HALLOWEEN WE WOULD BE BRAVE AND DON CREEPY
OUTFITS AND GO DOOR TO DOOR FOR CANDY AND COOKIES
AFTER DARK. MY MOTHER WOULD BAKE GINGERSNAPS
FOR THE TRICK-OR-TREATERS, AND THE ENTIRE
HOUSE WOULD SMELL LIKE THEM. AT DINNER WE'D
EAT COLCANNON, WHICH IS SIMILAR TO "BOERENKOOL,"
A CLASSIC DUTCH ONE-POT MEAL OF MASHED POTATOES
AND KALE. WE WOULD HIDE A GOLDEN RING, A COIN, AND
A THIMBLE OR BUTTON IN THE COLCANNON: THE
PERSON WHO FOUND THE RING WOULD MARRY
WITHIN THE YEAR; THE COIN MEANT WEALTH;
THE THIMBLE OR BUTTON MEANT A SAD
EXISTENCE AS A BACHELOR OR SPINSTER.
SO: PRETTY EXCITING FOOD.

colcannon

FOR THE COLCANNON
1 lb (500 g) kale or green cabbage
salt
2 lb (1 kg) potatoes, peeled
2 or 3 leeks
½ cup plus 2 tbsp (150 ml) milk or
    cream
freshly grated nutmeg
freshly ground black pepper

FOR SERVING
7 tbsp (100 g) (salted!) butter
a ring
a coin
a button

Remove the tough stems from the kale. Coarsely chop the leaves and boil them in salted water until al dente, 10 to 15 minutes. In the meantime, boil the potatoes until tender. When the kale is done, drain it thoroughly and chop the leaves more finely. Cut the leeks into circles, rinse them thoroughly, then simmer them in a saucepan with the milk until tender, about 7 minutes.

Drain the potatoes, mash them, and stir in the braised leeks and some of the milk—you might not need all of it, so add it a little at a time, until you have a nice chunky mash.

Fold the kale into the mashed potatoes and season with nutmeg, salt, and pepper.

To serve, melt the butter in a small saucepan. Hide the ring, coin, and button in the colcannon; if you wish, you can wrap each object in plastic wrap. Serve the colcannon with a little well in the middle for the butter. Serve the melted butter in a small jug alongside.

GINGERSNAPS
TOO GOOD TO PASS UP

BEAT 1 CUP + 2 TBSP (250 G) BUTTER WITH 1¼ CUPS (250 G) SUGAR UNTIL CREAMY & WHITE. BEAT IN ½ CUP (125 ML) GOLDEN SYRUP, MAPLE SYRUP OR HONEY...

SIFT IN 4 CUPS (500 G) SELF-RISING FLOUR 2 TBSP GROUND GINGER 1 TBSP GROUND CINNAMON & A PINCH OF SALT. BEAT TO MAKE A SMOOTH BATTER

WITH 2 SPOONS, MAKE LITTLE HEAPS THE SIZE OF A WALNUT & FLATTEN THEM A LITTLE

BAKE IN A PREHEATED OVEN AT 300°F (150°C / GAS 2) UNTIL GOLDEN. ABOUT 25 MINUTES. LET COOL COMPLETELY

croquettes

My friend Guusje is as fond of croquettes as I am, and she's very skilled at making them herself. This recipe will yield a large quantity, as it's a shame to make only a few. Simply freeze the rest of 'em. You can deep fry them straight from the freezer, as it's done in the snack bar—just fry them a little longer, 6 or 7 minutes. Guus will show us how. Stay tuned.

FOR 15 TO 20 CROQUETTES (OR 30 TO 40 SMALLER *BITTERBALLEN*, DUTCH APPETIZERS)

FOR THE BROTH
1 lb (500 g) boneless beef stew meat
1 large carrot, coarsely chopped
¼ celeriac, coarsely chopped
a few fresh thyme sprigs
2 bay leaves
1 onion, halved (with skin)
a few black peppercorns
salt to taste

FOR THE CROQUETTE MIXTURE
1 onion, diced
3 tbsp (50 g) butter
⅓ cup (50 g) all-purpose flour
¼ cup plus 3 tbsp (100 ml) sherry
    (I use medium-sweet)
1 small bunch fresh parsley, chopped
salt and freshly ground black pepper
freshly grated nutmeg

FOR BREADING
all-purpose flour
5 or 6 eggs, beaten
plain toasted or dry bread crumbs
vegetable oil, for deep-frying

FOR SERVING
soft white bread
prepared hot mustard

Make the broth: Place all the ingredients for the broth in a large saucepan with 4½ cups (1 l) cold water. Bring to a boil, then lower the heat and simmer for about 2 hours, until the meat is very tender. Strain the broth into a bowl and set it aside. Remove the beef from the strainer and discard the vegetables. Chop the beef and set it aside.

Make the croquette mixture: In a small saucepan, saute the onion in the butter over medium heat until soft; don't let it brown. Add the flour and stir for a bit. Add the sherry and whisk in 2 cups (½ l) of the broth.

Add the chopped beef and the parsley and season with salt, pepper, and nutmeg.

Allow the mixture to cool, then refrigerate it until completely chilled, preferably overnight.

Fry the croquettes: Form long rounded logs from the croquette mixture and cut them into lengths of about 3 inches (8 cm), or half that size for bitterballen. Don't make the logs too thick, or they will take too long to fry and the crust will become too dark. Put out three deep plates, one filled with flour, one with the beaten eggs, and one filled with bread crumbs. Roll the croquettes first in the flour, then in the egg, and then in the bread crumbs. Dip again in the egg and finally in the bread crumbs for a beautiful, firm crust. Place the croquettes on a baking sheet and refrigerate again for 30 minutes.

In a heavy pot, heat 2 inches of oil to 350°F (180°C).

Deep-fry the croquettes until golden brown, about 4 minutes. Drain on paper towels and serve with bread and mustard.

ricotta cheesecake with lemon syrup

FOR THE CRUST

1 box of crisp, crumbly cookies, like
    graham crackers (about 20)
¼ cup (60 g) packed light brown
    sugar
1 tbsp flour
pinch of salt
5 tbsp (75 g) butter, melted

FOR THE FILLING

2 cups (400 g) ricotta, drained for a
    few hours in a sieve
2 cups (400 g) mascarpone, at room
    temperature
seeds from 1 vanilla bean
1 cup (200 g) superfine sugar
grated zest of 1 lemon
pinch of salt
4 eggs

FOR THE SYRUP

¾ cup (2 dl) freshly squeezed
    lemon juice (that's from
    2 or 3 lemons)
½ cup plus 2 tbsp (125 g) superfine
    sugar

Make the crust: Preheat the oven to 350°F (180°C) and position the rack in the center.

Grind the cookies to fine crumbs and mix with the brown sugar, flour, and salt—this is easiest in a food processor. Add the butter and, if the mixture isn't moist enough to clump, 1 to 2 tbsp water. Butter a 9½-inch (24-cm) springform pan and line the bottom with a round of parchment paper. Press the crumbly mixture evenly over the bottom, and also push it up the sides.

Bake the crust until it begins to color, about 15 minutes. Let cool.

You can do all this a day in advance, just cover the crust and keep it at room temperature.

Make the filling: Preheat the oven to 325°F (160°C). Wrap the outside of the springform pan very tightly with aluminum foil. This will ensure that no water can seep into the cake from the water bath.

Gather up the towel containing the ricotta and squeeze it carefully to release any remaining liquid. With a mixer, beat the mascarpone until smooth. Add the drained ricotta and beat thoroughly. Add the vanilla bean seeds, superfine sugar, lemon zest, and salt and beat until smooth. Beat in the eggs one at the time.

Pour the filling into the crust and place the springform pan in a larger roasting pan. Put this in the oven and fill the roasting pan with hot water to come halfway up the sides of the springform pan.

Bake for about 1½ hours, or until the center is firm; you can test this by gently shaking the pan.

Let the cheesecake cool on a rack, then put in the refrigerator to firm up.

Make the syrup: Boil the lemon juice with the sugar until you have a clear, thickish syrup. Let cool.

Remove the sides of the springform pan and cut the cheesecake into wedges with a long thin knife. Pour lemon syrup on top of each piece and serve.

QUINOA APPLE CAKE

BOIL 1 CUP. (170G) QUINOA IN WATER FOR 10 MIN. UNTIL TENDER. DRAIN THOROUGHLY

MIX WITH

1 CUP (125G) SELF-RISING FLOUR

2 APPLES IN CHUNKS

3/4 CUP (125G) PACKED BROWN SUGAR

3/4 CUP (125G) RAISINS

7 TBSP (100 G) BUTTER, MELTED

AND SPICES:
1 TSP OF EACH
· GROUND CINNAMON
· GROUND GINGER
· FRESHLY GRATED NUTMEG
· + A PINCH OF SALT

PREHEAT THE OVEN TO 350°F (175°C/GAS 4).
PLACE A RACK JUST BELOW THE CENTER OF THE OVEN
POUR THE MIXTURE INTO A GREASED LOAF PAN
(YOU COULD LINE THE BOTTOM WITH PARCHMENT—I WOULD)
BAKE FOR ABOUT 50 MIN. UNTIL BROWN.
EAT WHILE IT'S STILL WARM!

FOR 2 SMALL JARS (ABOUT 2 CUPS) **1. set** out on the counter: 1 cup (100 g) chopped hazelnuts, ⅔ cup (100 g) almonds, ⅔ cup (100 g) peanuts, 1 tsp cinnamon, pinch of salt, 2 to 3 tbsp sugar (to taste), 1 tbsp apple syrup (Dutch *appelstroop*; use molasses or honey if you can't find it), and ¼ cup plus 2 tbsp (1 dl) sunflower oil. **2. put** everything in a food processor. **3. grind** thoroughly, or really as finely as you like. If the paste turns out a little dry, you can add some more oil. **4. spoon** into clean jars; it will keep for weeks in the fridge, but you won't have it around that long.

nut butter

Oh, nut paste or peanut butter, it's really damn good! It's easy to make yourself—there's nothing to it. Not only can you choose your favorite nuts for this, but you can also add chocolate to make homemade Nutella. Or you could add some chiles for a spicy nut butter; it's completely up to you.

I only see good things coming. Get to work!

ridiculously delicious mudcake with homemade nut butter

No exaggeration: This may be the best recipe for the best chocolate cake. We're talking pure chocolate indulgence.

Instead of homemade nut butter you can use Nutella, plain peanut butter, whipped cream, or nothing. Whatever works for you.

Serve warm with the salty caramel sauce from the salty sticky toffee puddings on page 228 and vanilla ice cream.

1 cup (250 ml) milk

2¼ cups (450 g) sugar

1 cup plus 2 tbsp (250 g) butter, cut into pieces

5¼ oz (150 g) very dark chocolate, chopped

2 eggs

⅓ cup plus 2 tbsp (100 ml) whiskey or rum

½ cup plus 2 tbsp (75 g) self-rising flour

1 cup (125 g) all-purpose flour

1¼ cups (100 g) unsweetened cocoa powder, plus extra for garnish

pinch of salt

1 jar nut butter (page 54) per layer of filling (for this cake I used 2 jars)

Preheat the oven to 325°F (160°C). If you have a convection oven, don't turn on the fan or the cake will become too dry.

Heat the milk with the sugar in a medium saucepan, but don't let it boil! Stir in the butter a little at a time. Once the butter has melted, add the chocolate the same way. Remove from the heat and let stand, stirring occasionally, until the chocolate has melted.

Grease a 9-inch (22-cm) round cake pan and put a round of parchment paper in the bottom. Line the sides with a strip of parchment paper as well, and make sure the edges stick up above the rim. Grease the parchment paper. The batter is pretty liquid, so it's best to use a closed pan. If you do use a springform pan or a cake pan with a removable bottom, put it on a small baking sheet in case it leaks.

Beat the eggs with the whiskey and, while stirring, pour the egg mixture into the warm chocolate mixture. Sift the self-rising flour with the all-purpose flour, the cocoa, and the salt into a big bowl. Pour the melted chocolate mixture into the flour mixture, stirring until combined, then pour the batter into the prepared cake pan.

Bake the cake for 1½ hours, or until a toothpick inserted in the center comes out dry and clean.

Let the cake cool in the pan for 10 minutes, then turn it out onto a rack and let it cool completely.

Split the cake in half horizontally—or, if you dare, into more layers—and spread each interior layer generously with the nut butter. Assemble the layers and sift cocoa powder on top before serving.

Eat nothing else all day.

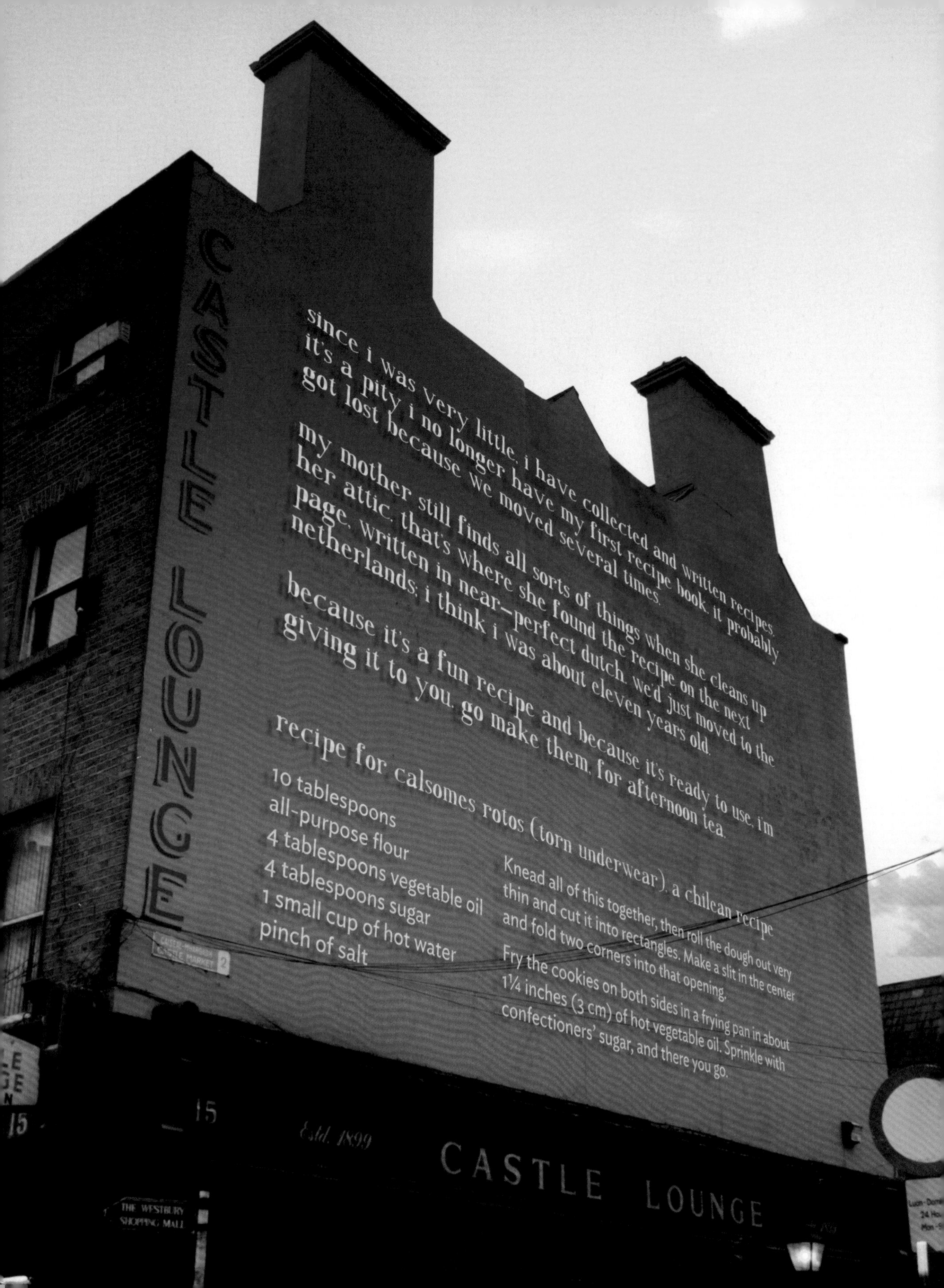
CASTLE LOUNGE
since i was very little, i have collected and written recipes.
it's a pity i no longer have my first recipe book. it probably
got lost because we moved several times.
my mother still finds all sorts of things when she cleans up
her attic. that's where she found the recipe on the next
page, written in near–perfect dutch. we'd just moved to the
netherlands; i think i was about eleven years old.
because it's a fun recipe and because it's ready to use, i'm
giving it to you. go make them, for afternoon tea.
recipe for calsomes rotos (torn underwear), a chilean recipe
10 tablespoons
all-purpose flour
4 tablespoons vegetable oil
4 tablespoons sugar
1 small cup of hot water
pinch of salt
Knead all of this together, then roll the dough out very
thin and cut it into rectangles. Make a slit in the center
and fold two corners into that opening.
Fry the cookies on both sides in a frying pan in about
1¼ inches (3 cm) of hot vegetable oil. Sprinkle with
confectioners' sugar, and there you go.
15
15
Estd. 1899
CASTLE LOUNGE
THE WESTBURY
SHOPPING MALL

Recept van (Gla) Calsomes Rotos (kapotte onderbroekjes) een Chileens recept

10 eetlepels bloem.
4 eetlepels olie
4 eetlepels suiker
1 klein kopje heet water.
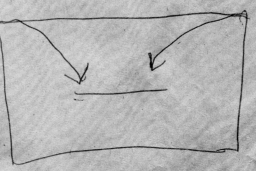

een beetje zout.

Dit allemaal door elkaar kneden, het deeg héél dun uitrollen, van het deeg recht-hoeken snyden, in 't midden een snee maken te twee punten door de opening vouwen het koekje bakken in de koekepan. met hete olie (een laag van ± 3 cm) aan 2 kanten bruin laten bakken. poeder suiker erover heen en en klaar is kees.

pecan caramel tart

FOR THE DOUGH

1½ cups (200 g) all-purpose flour

½ cup (100 g) sugar

7 tbsp (100 g) butter

1 egg

pinch of salt

FOR THE FILLING

1¼ cups (125 g) pecan halves

3 eggs

3 tbsp (50 g) butter, melted

¾ cup (150 g) packed light brown
    sugar

⅓ cup plus 2 tbsp (150 g) golden
    syrup or light corn syrup

3 tbsp plus 1 tsp (50 ml) heavy cream

Make the dough: Combine the dry ingredients, then cut in the butter until the texture resembles a coarse meal. Add the egg and swiftly knead to make a smooth dough. Place it in the fridge for half an hour, wrapped in plastic. Preheat the oven to 350°F (175°C).

Roll out the dough on a floured countertop. Place the dough in a greased 9½-inch or 10½-inch (24-cm or 26-cm) round tart pan, preferably one with a removable bottom (I've used a square one for this picture, but a round one will do the job perfectly). Cut off the extra dough at the edges.

Make the filling: Briefly toast the nuts in a dry skillet over medium heat. Let them cool completely.

Quickly whisk together the remaining filling ingredients and pour into the dough-lined tart pan. Arrange the nuts neatly over the filling and very carefully put the tart in the oven.

Bake about 30 minutes, until golden brown. The filling will still feel gooey, but it will solidify as it cools. The tart may also become quite fluffy in the oven, but it will flatten out over time. Let the tart cool completely before slicing.

chocolate nutmeg cupcakes & glossy coffee frosting

FOR 12 CUPCAKES

½ cup plus 2 tbsp (150 g) butter
1 cup plus 2 tbsp (225 g) sugar
2 eggs
1¼ cups (150 g) self-rising flour
1 tsp freshly grated nutmeg
¼ cup (30 g) unsweetened cocoa
    powder
1 packet (2 tsp) vanilla sugar
pinch of salt
½ cup plus 2 tbsp (150 ml) milk or
    buttermilk
4½ oz (120 g) dark chocolate,
    chopped small enough to mix
    easily into the batter (optional,
    for cupcakes with intense
    chocolate nuggets inside)

FOR THE FROSTING
¾ cup (150 g) packed dark brown
    sugar
½ cup plus 2 tbsp (50 g)
    unsweetened cocoa powder
¼ cup plus 2 tbsp (50 g) cornstarch
pinch of salt
1 sachet (2 tsp) instant espresso
    powder
1 packet (2 tsp) vanilla sugar
3 tbsp (50 g) butter

Make the cupcakes: Preheat the oven to 350°F (180°C). Position the rack in the center of the oven. Line a muffin tin with paper liners.

Using a hand mixer, beat the butter and sugar in a big bowl until the mixture is light and airy. Beat in the eggs one at the time. In another bowl, combine the flour, nutmeg, cocoa powder, vanilla sugar, and salt. Alternate beating the flour mixture and the milk into the butter mixture until just incorporated; don't mix for too long.

Add the chocolate chunks, gently folding them into the batter.

Divide the batter among the muffin cups. Bake 25 to 30 minutes, until a toothpick inserted in a cupcake comes out dry. Let cool for 5 minutes, then lift the cupcakes out of the tin and let cool completely on a rack.

Make the frosting: In a medium saucepan, combine the brown sugar, cocoa powder, cornstarch, salt, espresso powder, and vanilla sugar. Stir in ¾ cup (200 ml) water. Over low heat, bring to a boil, stirring occasionally. Once the mixture begins to boil, stir continuously to prevent it from burning.

Boil the frosting for 1 full minute. Remove from the heat and stir in the butter. Dip the top of each cupcake in the frosting, twist slightly, lift up, and let cool until set.

EPIPHANY

JANUARY 6 IS EPIPHANY,
OR THREE KINGS DAY. IT'S CELEBRATED IN THE
SOUTH OF THE NETHERLANDS, AND EVEN MORE SO
IN FRANCE. THEY CALL IT "L'EPIPHANIE." AFTER CHRISTMAS,
YOU'LL SEE SPECIAL CAKES IN ALL THE WINDOWS OF PARISIAN
BAKERIES: "GALETTES DES ROIS." THEY LOOK A LITTLE LIKE THE
TYPICAL DUTCH ALMOND-FILLED SHORTBREAD, AND THEY'RE EATEN
THROUGHOUT JANUARY. HIDDEN IN EACH CAKE IS A "FÈVE," A BEAN.
THE PERSON WHO FINDS THE BEAN IS VERY LUCKY: HE OR SHE WILL
BE KING THAT DAY. AND THAT'S WHY THERE'S ALSO A PAPER
CROWN SOLD WITH EVERY CAKE. I WAS LUCKY: WHEN I GOT MY
FIRST PIECE OF THIS CAKE, FROM MONIQUE, IN PARIS, I FOUND THE BEAN!
(THOUGH I DO SUSPECT MONIQUE PUT IT IN MY PIECE ON PURPOSE.)

galette des rois

FOR THE CRÈME PÂTISSIÈRE
½ cup (125 ml) milk
1 sachet (2 tsp) vanilla sugar
1 egg yolk
1 tbsp granulated sugar
1 tbsp all-purpose flour or
    cornstarch

FOR THE ALMOND FILLING
3 tbsp (50 g) butter, at room
    temperature
⅓ cup (75 g) sugar
1 egg
1 cup (100 g) ground almonds
a few drops of bitter-almond extract
    (you can get a really good one in
    specialty stores)

FOR THE DOUGH
1 lb (450 g) frozen puff pastry
flour, for dusting

AND FURTHER
1 *fève*: the bean
If you can't get a real French one
    made of porcelain (which, by
    the way, doesn't look like a bean
    at all), then just use a large
    dried bean
1 egg yolk
1 golden crown made of cardboard

Make the crème pâtissière: In a saucepan, bring the milk and vanilla sugar almost to a boil. In a bowl, beat the egg yolk with the granulated sugar and flour until foamy and smooth. While stirring, add the warm milk to the egg mixture and then pour everything back into the saucepan.

Bring this slowly to a boil, stirring constantly, and let the crème thicken; it should be like yogurt. Remove from the heat and let cool. Press plastic wrap directly onto the surface of the crème (so you won't get milk skin—yuck) and set aside until use.

Make the almond filling: Beat the butter with the sugar until smooth, then add the egg, almonds, and extract. Stir ½ cup (100 g) of the crème pâtissière into the almond mixture. The result, in French, is called frangipane. Refrigerate the frangipane until use. I prefer to do this because it allows the frangipane to stiffen. The recipe can be made to this point one day in advance.

Preheat the oven to 350°F (180°C).

Thaw the puff pastry and roll it out on a lightly floured surface into a big rectangle. Using a plate as a guide, cut out 2 circles of about 9 inches (24 cm) in diameter.

Place one of the circles on a baking sheet and spread the frangipane over the circle, leaving about 1 inch (2.5 cm) clear at the edge. Don't forget to hide the bean in it!

Beat the egg yolk and brush it onto the clear edge of the pastry. Place the second circle on top and press the edges together firmly.

Brush the rest of the egg yolk over the top and lightly score a pattern of diamonds or sun rays on top with a knife.

Bake the pie for 25 to 30 minutes, until golden brown.

Let it cool slightly, and ask the youngest person around to cut the pie into equal pieces.

He who finds the bean will be king that day: Crown him!

guinness fruitcake

FOR THE CAKE: 3½ CUPS (450 G) SELF-RISING FLOUR • 2 TSP GROUND CINNAMON • 1 TSP FRESHLY GRATED NUTMEG • 1 TSP GROUND GINGER • 1 CUP (225 G) BUTTER, IN SMALL CHUNKS • ⅔ CUP (100 G) CURRANTS • ⅔ CUP (100 G) GOLDEN RAISINS • ⅔ CUP (100 G) CANDIED PEEL • GRATED ZEST OF 1 LEMON • 1 CUP + 2 TBSP (250 G) PACKED BROWN SUGAR • ¾ CUP + 1 TBSP (200 ML) GUINNESS OR ANOTHER STOUT • 4 EGGS, BEATEN • FOR SERVING (OPTIONAL): CONFECTIONERS' SUGAR • SOME EXTRA GUINNESS • UNSWEETENED WHIPPED CREAM OR SALTED BUTTER

PREHEAT THE OVEN TO 325°F (160°C). (IF YOU HAVE A CONVECTION OVEN, TURN OFF THE FAN.) • GREASE A 9-INCH (22-CM) ROUND CAKE PAN WITH A REMOVABLE BOTTOM AND LINE THE BOTTOM AND SIDES WITH PARCHMENT PAPER. GREASE THE PARCHMENT PAPER. • SIFT THE FLOUR WITH THE SPICES INTO A BIG BOWL. USE A FORK TO QUICKLY RUB THE BUTTER CHUNKS INTO THE FLOUR MIXTURE UNTIL IT LOOKS LIKE COARSE BREAD CRUMBS. ADD THE CURRANTS, RAISINS, CANDIED PEEL, LEMON ZEST, AND BROWN SUGAR AND MIX WELL. • BEAT THE GUINNESS INTO THE EGGS AND TRICKLE THIS INTO THE FLOUR MIXTURE, STIRRING UNTIL COMBINED. POUR INTO THE PREPARED CAKE PAN AND SMOOTH THE TOP. • BAKE FOR 1 HOUR. LOWER THE OVEN TEMPERATURE TO JUST UNDER 300°F (140°C) AND LOOSELY COVER THE CAKE WITH ALUMINUM FOIL. BAKE FOR ANOTHER HOUR, UNTIL A TOOTHPICK INSERTED IN THE CENTER COMES OUT DRY. • LET THE CAKE COOL ON A RACK. TO SERVE, SPRINKLE CONFECTIONERS' SUGAR ON TOP OR PRICK SOME HOLES IN THE CAKE AND DRIZZLE A LITTLE GUINNESS OVER IT. SERVE WITH WHIPPED CREAM OR SALTED BUTTER.

Glendalough

Schellingwoude

Amsterdam

Powerscourt

cardamom cake with whole pears & white chocolate

This recipe has been published all over in magazines and newspapers, but I really don't care; since it's so good and it looks so cool, it belongs in this collection.

Make it, and you're sold.

FOR THE PEARS

3 medium-size crisp, firm pears
(such as Bosc), peeled but
whole, with the stem left on
1 (750-ml) bottle dry white wine
1¼ cups (250 g) sugar
4 cloves
3 star anise
8 cardamom pods
2 cinnamon sticks

FOR THE CAKE

1½ cups plus 2 tbsp (200 g) butter,
softened, plus extra for greasing
1 cup (200 g) sugar
4 eggs
1½ cups (200 g) self-rising flour
1 generous tbsp ground cardamom
pinch of salt

AND FURTHER

3 oz (90 g) white chocolate, in chunks

Poach the pears: In a large saucepan, combine the pears, wine, sugar, cloves, star anise, cardamom, and cinnamon and poach for 30 minutes over low heat.

Take the pears out of the liquid and set aside to cool. Add 2½ cups (500 ml) water to the poaching liquid and boil to reduce the liquid by half. Let cool.

Make the cake: Preheat the oven to 350°F (170°C).

Using a hand mixer, beat the butter and sugar in a large bowl until creamy. Beat in the eggs one at the time. Don't add a new egg until the previous one is incorporated.

Sift the flour, cardamom, and salt over the batter and fold it in.

Butter a 9-by-5-inch (1.5 l) loaf pan and line it with parchment paper. Butter the parchment paper.

Spoon the batter into the pan. Press the pears in, stem end up. Bake for 40 minutes, until a toothpick inserted into the cake part comes out clean.

Allow to cool in the pan, then gently remove the cake from the pan to a rack to cool completely.

Very carefully melt the chocolate: Set a heatproof bowl over a pan of simmering water, making sure the bowl doesn't touch the water. Stir the chocolate in the bowl until melted. Using a spoon, drizzle the chocolate over the cake and create nice stripes on top.

Let the chocolate dry for a bit and serve the cake in thick slices, with the reduced pear syrup poured on top.

joanna's cornflake chocolate chunkies

In my last book I wrote about Joanna, a friend of my mother's, who is an excellent cook and from whom I've learned a lot. Her "tea parties" were inimitable, from my perspective as a child. I would always try them at home and I'd often call Joanna for new recipes. She wrote down many of them. Recently, when I went over for dinner, I came home with a few new ones. She knows how happy they make me.

When I was a child, this was one of my favorite treats. I can still see them on the kitchen table and now, because I still love them, I am passing the recipe to you.

FOR ABOUT 12 PIECES

½ cup (120 g) butter
¼ cup golden syrup or light corn
    syrup
¼ cup unsweetened cocoa powder
¼ cup confectioners' sugar
¼ cup raisins or other dried fruit
    such as cherries or cranberries
3 to 4 handfuls of cornflakes or rice
    krispies

Melt the butter with the syrup in a medium saucepan over low heat. Stir in the cocoa powder and remove from the heat.

Stir in the confectioners' sugar, raisins, and cornflakes.

Stir gently, until everything is fully coated in the syrup mixture. If there's a lot of syrup mixture left, add more cornflakes.

Set cupcake papers or a sheet of parchment paper out on the counter.

Using two spoons, spoon two heaps of the mixture in every cup. Let harden completely and attack.

flapjacks

Flapjacks are English or Irish, slightly chewy oatmeal bars, similar to granola bars. This is a basic recipe, but once you've succeeded with the first batch, you'll likely find yourself experimenting. You can add chopped dried fruit, for example, or nuts, like pine nuts, or chunks of chocolate.

FOR ABOUT 12 PIECES

½ cup plus 1 tbsp (125 g) butter
½ cup plus 2 tbsp (125 g) packed
    brown sugar
¼ cup plus 2 tbsp (125 g) honey or
    golden syrup
3 cups (250 g) rolled oats
pinch of salt

Preheat the oven to 325°F (160°C).

Line an 8-inch (20-cm) square baking pan with parchment paper.

Melt the butter in a medium saucepan over low heat. Add the brown sugar and honey and stir until the sugar has dissolved.

Stir the oats into the butter mixture. Spoon into the baking pan and flatten the mixture with the back of a wooden spatula.

Bake for about 30 minutes. The top should be golden brown, but you don't want to bake it too long; the flapjacks should be chewy and not acquire a burned taste.

Remove from the oven. Let cool for 5 minutes, then invert the pan onto a wooden cutting board to release the flapjacks. Cut into equal pieces and let cool completely. Store them in an airtight container.

CHOROLATE KRISPIES

4 ozs margarine
4 level tablespoons syrup (or
4 level tablespoons cocoa
4 level tablespoons icing sugar,
Sultanas - cherries - etc.
Rice krispies or Cornflakes.

Melt fat + syrup in a saucepan,
stir in cocoa - remove from heat
+ stir in icing sugar, fruit +
cornflakes - when well coated
put into paper cases + leave
to set.

"CLEEVE"

1/- Bar Cleeves
12 Marshma
4 ozs. mara
Melt
water. Add
tin to set .

73

Hippodrome, Prix d'Amerique Marionnaud, Paris

Georgian House, Dublin

ST. NICHOLAS'S EVE

DECEMBER 5 IS SINTERKLAAS,
OR ST. NICHOLAS'S EVE. WHEN I GREW UP IN IRELAND
WE WOULD CELEBRATE IT WITH OTHER DUTCH CHILDREN
IN THE PHILIPS OFFICE IN DUBLIN. THAT WAS COOL
BECAUSE WE WOULD LATER CELEBRATE CHRISTMAS AS WELL.
SO WE'D GET TWICE AS MANY PRESENTS IN DECEMBER.
BIG PACKAGES WOULD ARRIVE BY MAIL FROM THE NETHERLANDS
BECAUSE ST. NICHOLAS WAS OFTEN MISTAKEN AND HAD
BROUGHT THEM TO MY AUNTS AND UNCLES IN LIMBURG, WHO
WOULD HAVE TO FORWARD THEM TO US. WE'D ALSO GET
A LOT OF TYPICAL DUTCH SWEETS AND CANDIES BECAUSE
YOU COULDN'T GET THEM IN IRELAND. MY MOTHER WOULD
BAKE GINGER COOKIES, AND ST. NICHOLAS WOULD SEND
"TAAI TAAI," "PEPERNOTEN," BUTTER FUDGE, AND "GEVULDE
SPECULAAS"—SPICE BREAD FILLED WITH ALMOND PASTE.
MY MOTHER WOULD WOLF DOWN THE SPICE BREAD.
SHE SIMPLY LOVED IT.

sintercookies

FOR ABOUT 36 COOKIES,
DEPENDING ON THE SIZE

1½ cups (200 g) all-purpose flour
½ cup (100 g) sugar
pinch of salt
1½ tsp Chinese five-spice powder
    (star anise, black pepper, fennel,
    cloves, and cinnamon)
1 tbsp anise seeds, plus extra for
    garnish
6 tbsp (80 g) butter
2 to 3 tbsp crème fraîche
2 eggs, beaten

Combine all the dry ingredients in a large bowl. Cut in the butter until the mixture resembles a coarse meal, then add the crème fraîche and knead to make a smooth dough. Do it quickly; too much kneading will make for tough cookies. They should be crisp!

Let the dough rest in the refrigerator for 1 hour.

Preheat the oven to 350°F (180°C). Line two cookie sheets with parchment paper.

Roll the dough out ¼ inch (6 mm) thick on a lightly floured surface. Cut out cookies with a cookie cutter. Scrape the leftover dough together and repeat until all the dough is used. Place the cookies on the cookie sheets. Brush the cookies with the beaten egg and sprinkle with anise seeds.

Bake the cookies for 12 to 15 minutes, until golden brown. Let cool on a rack.

MAKING BUTTER FUDGE

STIR ½ CUP (100 G) LIGHT BROWN SUGAR INTO 3 TBS MILK & BRING TO A BOIL. QUICKLY ADD ½ CUP (50 G) CONFECTIONERS' SUGAR TO THE MIXTURE AND STIR. (ADD FOOD COLORING IF YOU LIKE)

IMMEDIATELY POUR THE MIXTURE INTO A WELL-GREASED FORM THAT YOU HAVE PLACED ON TOP OF A SMOOTH, GREASED BASE.
→ IT HARDENS QUICKLY! YOU CAN REMOVE THE FORM ONCE WHITE DOTS APPEAR ON TOP.

TURN THE FUDGE ONTO ONE EDGE TO DRY COMPLETELY

gevulde speculaas: spice bread filled with almond paste

2 cups (250 g) self-rising flour
pinch of salt
1 tbsp ground allspice
¾ cup (150 g) packed light brown
    sugar
½ cup plus 2 tbsp (150 g) cold
    butter, cut into pieces
2 tbsp milk
10½ oz (300 g) almond paste
    (available in specialized pastry
    stores and some grocery stores)
⅓ cup (50 g) blanched almonds,
    halved
1 egg yolk

Sift the flour, salt, and allspice into a large bowl. Add the brown sugar, butter, and milk. Swiftly knead the mixture into a smooth dough. Refrigerate the dough for 1 hour.

Preheat the oven to 325°F (160°C). Butter an 8- or 9-inch (20- or 22-cm) square baking pan.

Divide the dough in half and roll out one half on a lightly floured surface to cover the bottom of the pan. Spread the almond paste evenly over the dough, leaving ½ inch (1 cm) free on all sides. Roll out the other half of the dough and arrange it squarely on top of the paste. Garnish the top with the almond halves and brush it with the egg yolk.

Bake for about 45 minutes, until golden brown. Let cool and cut into pieces.

1. put in a blender or food processor: ¾ cup (200 ml) heavy cream, 1 can (14 oz/400 ml) sweetened condensed milk, 1¼ cups (300 ml) Irish whiskey, 1 tbsp instant coffee granules, 2 tbsp chocolate syrup (Monin brand—I buy it in coffee and tea specialty stores). **2.** blend briefly, until it's just mixed. **3.** pour into clean bottles and close. Kept in the refrigerator, this will remain fresh for at least 2 months.

irish cream liqueur

It's almost easier than making tea! This recipe, for about 4½ cups (1 l), makes a pretty strong drink because that's how I like it. If it's too strong for you, simply cut down on the whiskey. Or fill your glass with lots of ice cubes.

Served over vanilla ice cream, this is awfully delicious.

hot whiskey

After a day outside in the cold, there's nothing that will warm you up like a big glass of hot whiskey. Completely soaked after a walk along the stormy coast, it was the only drink that would get me warm. Well . . . maybe it was also the fire in the fireplace and the tall tales from the men in the bar.

FOR 1 GLASS

a splash of Irish whiskey (you may
    add 1 to 2 tsp sugar, but I always
    do without)
2 or 3 cloves
1 or 2 slices of lemon
boiling water

Pour the whiskey into a heatproof glass. Stir in sugar, if you wish. Stick the cloves in the lemon slices, put them in the glass, and add boiling water until your glass is full.

Stir until the sugar is dissolved and drink.

mulled wine

The kick is in the gin—you'll see.

This is a good method for mulling wine, as the wine doesn't simmer for hours and evaporate—such a waste.

I got this recipe from someone and have now given it my own twist. Oh well, that's how it goes with recipes. You'll probably do the same.

FOR 8 TO 10 SERVINGS

2 (750-ml) bottles full-bodied red
    wine
5 tbsp sugar
juice and peel of 3 clementines
4 bay leaves
5 cloves
6 cardamom pods, crushed
freshly grated nutmeg
3 star anise
2 cinnamon sticks
about 1 tbsp (15 ml) gin per glass

Put about ½ bottle of the wine (no need to be very precise) in a large saucepan, along with the sugar and the clementine juice and peel. Add all the spices and simmer over low heat for 20 to 30 minutes.

Just before serving, add the rest of the wine.

Heat the wine until nearly boiling, then remove from the heat and let steep for about 5 minutes. Pour the wine into heatproof glasses or mugs and add a splash of gin to each.

apple cider

You probably didn't know it was this easy to make. And you don't even need much in the way of equipment. Do make sure to use only very clean pans and utensils, and rinse the bucket thoroughly.

You can drink the cider immediately. If you leave it in the fridge for a while it'll become more syrupy, but add some water or ice and it will be perfect. It could contain some alcohol from the fermenting process, so don't give it to your kids!

FOR ABOUT 3½ QUARTS (3 L) **1**. CUT 6½ lb (3 kg) apples (such as Empire or Gala, but any sweeter variety will be fine), into quarters. You can leave them unpeeled and cores intact—that's fine. **2**. grate all the apples with a coarse grater. It's easiest in a food processor. Well, easier, but it's actually pretty hard work. **3**. put all the grated apple in a clean plastic or enamel bucket and add 4½ cups (1 l) water. Cover with plastic wrap and stow in an out-of-the-way spot for 7 days. Under your desk, for example. **4**. stir the pulp once a day with a clean spoon and cover again. **5**. spoon the apples into a strainer placed

over a large bowl. **6. push** as much juice out of the pulp as possible with the back of a spoon, then throw the pulp out. **7. pour** the strained liquid back into the bucket. Add 2½ cups (500 g) sugar, 3 tbsp finely grated fresh ginger, and 3 cinnamon sticks. Stir until the sugar is dissolved. Cover and let stand for another day. **8. after** 1 day, pour everything through a piece of cheesecloth placed in a strainer over a large bowl. **9. let** it quietly seep through. Stir occasionally. **10. pull** up the edges of the cloth and wring gently until almost nothing seeps out anymore. Don't squeeze too hard or you'll have too

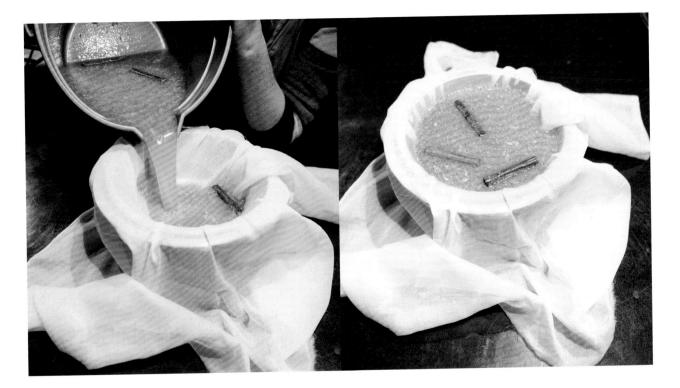

much sediment in your bottle. **11. pour** the cider through a funnel into sterilized bottles and close them with a screw cap. Don't fill them completely; leave some air in the bottle. Some gas will form and your bottle could burst if it's too full. You can drink the cider immediately, or you can save it in the fridge for a month or two—after 2 months you'll find it has quite a bit of effervescence! If it turns thicker or sweeter, just add some water.

snake bite

FOR 1 COCKTAIL

5 oz (150 ml) apple cider, sweet
    (pages 86–89)
5 oz (150 ml) light brown beer (I use
    a light Trappist like Chimay)

Pour the cider over the back of a spoon into the beer and serve immediately.

You could also use stout for this little cocktail to give it more of a knockout punch.

my leaf peeper

FOR 1 COCKTAIL

1 tbsp cinnamon
3 tbsp sugar
1½ oz (50 ml) vodka
3½ oz (100 ml) apple cider, sweet
    (pages 86–89), plus extra for
    the glass
½ tsp maple syrup

Fill a martini glass with ice cubes and swirl them to cool the glass.

Mix the cinnamon with the sugar and sprinkle it over a saucer.

Shake the vodka, cider, and syrup in a cocktail shaker filled with ice cubes. Remove the ice from the martini glass. Dip the edge of the glass in a shallow dish of apple cider, then dip it in the cinnamon sugar on the saucer.

Strain the cocktail into the glass and serve.

apple cider digestif

Don't forget, you can serve cocktails before but also after dinner. The following recipe is really fun for after.

FOR 2 COCKTAILS

1½ oz (50 ml) apple cider
    (pages 86–89)
1½ oz (50 ml) calvados
¾ oz (25 ml) brandy
juice of ½ lemon
1 tsp golden syrup or light corn syrup

Combine all the ingredients in an ice-filled cocktail shaker and stir. Strain the drink into two fancy glasses.

Serve after dinner, ice cold and with a strong espresso.

spicy cider warm–up drink

First take a long walk along the beach in a storm. Come home chattering and serve this warm-up drink: You won't even need a hot shower.

FOR 5 SERVINGS

4½ cups (1 l) apple cider, sweet
    (pages 86–89)
5 slices of orange
3 star anise
3 cloves
3 cinnamon sticks
1 cup (250 ml) dark rum

Heat the cider in a large saucepan over low heat and add the orange slices, star anise, cloves, and cinnamon sticks. Let steep for 30 minutes over low heat.

Remove from the heat and stir in the rum. Pour into thick heat-proof glasses and serve immediately.

winter cocktail

Snow and cranberries in a glass. It doesn't get any more wintry than this.

FOR 1 COCKTAIL

¾ oz (25 ml) vodka
1 big scoop (100 ml) vanilla ice
    cream
1 tsp very finely grated orange zest
1½ oz (50 ml) cranberry juice
3 to 5 fresh cranberries (optional)

Combine the vodka, ice cream, orange zest, and cranberry juice in a cocktail shaker and shake. Pour into a cocktail glass. Let stand briefly so the foam settles.

Garnish with fresh cranberries if you wish.

clementine negroni

Yes, a nice apéritif. Here are a few more ideas for a welcome drink to serve before a grand dinner, or at a party, or just because you feel like it.

THIS IS A RECIPE FOR 2 GLASSES:
1 FOR YOU AND 1 FOR THAT
OTHER PERSON. OR 2 GLASSES
FOR YOU ALONE.

4 clementines (peeled), plus 1 for
    garnish
1½ oz (50 ml) gin
1½ oz (50 ml) Campari
1½ oz (50 ml) dry vermouth

Place the peeled clementines in a blender and blend them into juice. Strain the juice into an ice-filled cocktail shaker and add the gin, Campari, and vermouth. Shake forcefully for 30 seconds. Strain into martini glasses and garnish with slices of clementine if you wish.

cranberry champagne

This recipe is for about 8, since once you open a bottle of Champagne it would be a waste not to use it all.

1 (750-ml) bottle Champagne or cava
8 oz (250 ml) cranberry juice
2 oz (60 ml) Cointreau
a handful of fresh mint leaves
a handful of fresh cranberries

In a big pitcher, combine the Champagne, cranberry juice, and Cointreau.

Pour into elegant glasses.

Garnish with mint leaves and fresh cranberries.

pineapple–ginger juice

Let's not forget to make something for the teetotalers among us. Make it well in advance, as the flavor will really improve with time.

If you do wish to spike it: A splash of vodka never goes wrong.

FOR 3 GLASSES

1 pineapple
a big chunk of fresh ginger, 2 or 3
    thumbs long
⅓ cup (75 g) turbinado or Demerara
    sugar

Peel and core the pineapple and chop it into small chunks. Don't worry about the eyes, as you'll strain the juice later on.

Peel the ginger and chop it into small chunks. Puree the pineapple with the ginger in a blender or food processor.

Add the sugar and ¾ cup (200 ml) water, stir, and set aside in the refrigerator for 4 hours.

Strain through a sieve into a big jug or pitcher, and with the back of a ladle push as much juice out of the pulp as possible.

Taste, and if needed, add more finely grated ginger.

Serve over ice in tall glasses.

DINNER IS READY!

But first, an apéritif. And something to snack on. Besides serving meat and cheese, olives, and such, I enjoy making something myself. After all, this is hard-core home made.

salt & vinegar crisps

4 medium-sized potatoes (about
    2¼ lb / 1 kg)
2 tbsp olive oil
1 tsp salt
freshly ground black pepper
cider vinegar or white wine vinegar

Preheat the oven to 350°F (170°C).

Wash the potatoes thoroughly but don't peel them.

Cut them into very thin slices using a mandoline or food processor. Pat the slices dry with paper towels. Sprinkle with the oil, salt, and pepper.

Line a couple of baking sheets with parchment paper and arrange the potato slices on them in a single layer. Bake about 12 minutes, until the bottoms turn golden brown. Sprinkle with vinegar and serve immediately.

spicy walnuts

1 cup plus 2 tbsp (225 g) sugar
1 tsp red pepper flakes
1 tsp ground ginger
1 tsp salt
3 tbsp soy sauce
1⅔ lb (750 g) walnuts

In a saucepan over low heat, heat the sugar with ⅓ cup (100 ml) water and stir until the sugar is dissolved. Bring to a boil, stirring. Let simmer for about 10 minutes, then remove from the heat.

Stir in the red pepper flakes, ginger, salt, and soy sauce, then add the nuts. Stir thoroughly to coat the nuts.

Line a baking sheet or serving tray with parchment paper.

Spread out the nut mixture on the baking sheet. Use the back of a spoon dipped in some oil to spread the nuts more easily. Let cool completely.

Break the nuts into bite-sized chunks and serve with a beer.

They'll keep for up to a week in a zip-top bag, but they won't last that long anyway.

I don't know about you, but at home we used to get popcorn as a snack. Popping corn was reason for a feast. You couldn't buy much in Ireland, but you could buy colored kernels for popping. I've never seen that anywhere else. I bought it again recently in Dublin, colored and black kernels, also very cool. Be creative and do something other than just throwing salt or sugar over it. I'll give you a hand.

lemon & dill popcorn

1 scant cup (100 g) popping corn
2 tbsp sunflower oil
1 tsp dill seed or dried dill
2 tbsp finely grated lemon zest
1 tsp paprika
½ tsp salt, or to taste
freshly ground black pepper

Pop the corn in small batches, never more than what comfortably fits in a single layer in the bottom of a large saucepan. The popcorn will expand to take up 8 times as much space!

Keep a lid nearby and heat the kernels in the oil over high heat. As soon as a few kernels start popping, put the lid on the pan and shake firmly. NEVER peek in the pan while the corn is popping. Remove from the heat once it becomes silent for a few seconds—don't wait until the popping has stopped completely or the rest will burn.

Put the popcorn in a large bowl.

In a mortar, grind the dill seeds coarsely, and sprinkle them, along with the lemon zest, paprika, salt, and pepper, over the popcorn.

popcorn rocks

1 scant cup (100 g) popping corn
2 tbsp sunflower oil
½ cup plus 2 tbsp (150 ml) pancake syrup (maple syrup is thinner, but you could use that)
½ tsp cinnamon
1 tsp red pepper flakes, or to taste
½ tsp salt, or to taste
1 tbsp butter
2 tbsp sesame seeds

Pop the corn in the oil as described on the previous page. Put the popcorn in a large bowl.

Heat the syrup with the cinnamon, red pepper flakes, and salt in a small saucepan. Bring to a boil, boil softly for about 2 minutes, then stir in the butter. WATCH OUT! It can splatter and it's really hot!

Pour about half of the caramel over the popcorn in the big bowl, swiftly stirring the popcorn around so it's all coated. Sprinkle with the sesame seeds. Continue turning the popcorn, and pour the rest of the caramel over it.

Spoon small heaps of popcorn onto a large baking sheet lined with parchment paper, and let them cool. Serve with beer.

ossenworst
(cured beef sausage)

This is my cousin and partner, Joris. Together we own the restaurant Aan de Amstel, but that's not important now because Joris and two of his friends also own De Eerste Hollandsche Worst Maatschappij, the First Dutch Sausage Company. They fry sausages at the swellest barbecues you've ever seen and at every location you could imagine. I couldn't find a better person to show you how ridiculously easy it is to make ossenworst yourself. Get to work!

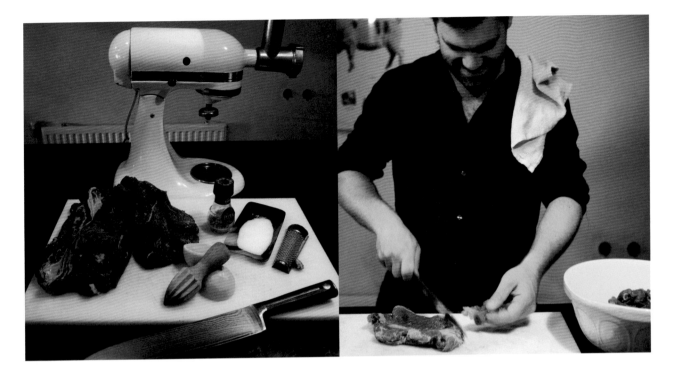

1. **place** 2¼ lb (1 kg) lean and 2¼ lb (1 kg) marbled chuck beef in the freezer 2 hours in advance, so that it's very cold. Ideally it's 34°F (1°C). But you don't need to be that precise. Further you'll need: 1 tsp (5 g) curing salt with 6.25% sodium nitrite (a.k.a. pink salt; you can get this from your local butcher or online), juice of ½ lemon, 1½ tbsp ground white pepper, and 2 tsp freshly grated nutmeg. 2. **cut** the fatty parts from the beef—the firm white parts. 3. **grind** all the beef as coarsely as possible in a meat grinder or food processor. 4. **add** the curing salt, lemon juice, pepper, and nutmeg. 5. **use** your hands to swiftly combine the ingredients: The meat shouldn't become warm. Tip from Joris: If your phone rings, put the meat back

in the freezer. **6. grind** everything again, but now more finely. If you have a meat grinder, it should be 3 to 5 mm. You'll see the meat turn darker, which is normal: The nitrite does that. Tomorrow it will be red again. **7. push** an artificial casing (you can buy these from your local butcher) around the nozzle of the meat grinder. Let the meat slide into the casing, but hold it tight and make sure no air gets in. Do it with a partner: One person firmly holds the casing, the other pushes the meat through. **8. bind** the sausages tightly. Let them rest for 24 hours in the fridge to solidify. (They'll keep for 2 weeks in the refrigerator.) Yes, you eat this sausage raw—it has been salted well enough to keep for 2 weeks. It's a bit like steak tartare.

mariëtte's sausage buns

This is one of the oldest recipes I have. It's my mother's recipe for sausage buns.

Every year, for as long as I can remember, my mother would make an enormous number of these sausage buns at the beginning of the Christmas holiday. If any made it to the holiday she'd freeze the extras, but usually they were gone long before Christmas and she would bake some more.

This was an easy way for her to serve snacks during the vacation, as we could heat them up ourselves in the oven. And just after Christmas, when we didn't crave fancy food anymore, we would eat them, wrapped in a paper napkin, while watching a Christmas movie on the couch.

These sausage buns are not just awfully delicious; for me they also taste like spending the day in your pajamas on the sofa. Years later I opened a restaurant with my cousin Joris and we put my mother's sausage buns on the lunch menu. They became an instant hit and have been there ever since. If you cut them into smaller pieces they can serve as an hors d'oeuvre.

Well, here's the recipe.

FOR 15 BUNS

FOR THE FILLING
2¼ lb (1 kg) ground sirloin
1 egg
3 tbsp ketchup
⅓ cup (75 ml) ketjap manis
   (Indonesian sweet soy sauce;
   available at Asian grocery stores)
1 tbsp Worcestershire sauce
1 tbsp cinnamon
1 tbsp allspice
1 tsp freshly grated nutmeg
2 tbsp prepared mustard
handful of dried bread crumbs
dash of Tabasco sauce
1 tsp salt

TO WRAP AND BAKE
oil or butter, for greasing
15 sheets frozen puff pastry, thawed
1 egg, beaten

Make the filling: Combine all the ingredients for the filling in a big bowl and mix thoroughly with your hands. For the bread crumbs, add as much as necessary to make the filling nicely consistent: not too moist, but smooth and not sticky.

Preheat the oven to 350°F (180°C). Grease one or two baking sheets or line with parchment paper.

For every sheet of pastry, form a "sausage" of the ground meat mixture. Fold the pastry around the meat and press the edge firmly with your fingertips, then crimp with a fork. Continue until all the meat and puff pastry sheets are used.

Arrange the rolls on the prepared baking sheets and brush them with the egg. Bake 25 to 30 minutes, until golden brown.

Eat them with mustard or with the apple & tomato chutney on page 37.

MINI GOAT CHEESE FONDUE

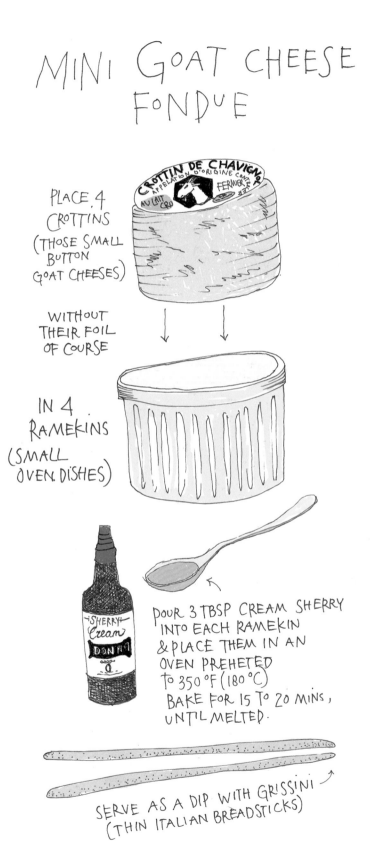

PLACE 4 CROTTINS (THOSE SMALL BUTTON GOAT CHEESES)

WITHOUT THEIR FOIL OF COURSE

IN 4 RAMEKINS (SMALL OVEN DISHES)

POUR 3 TBSP CREAM SHERRY INTO EACH RAMEKIN & PLACE THEM IN AN OVEN PREHETED TO 350°F (180°C) BAKE FOR 15 TO 20 MINS, UNTIL MELTED.

SERVE AS A DIP WITH GRISSINI (THIN ITALIAN BREADSTICKS)

butternut crème with goat cheese cream & sage

For 20 small glasses. It's quite a lot, I know. But it's really nice for a small party. The soup freezes well, but the goat cheese cream doesn't. If you serve the soup warm in regular bowls, it's enough to serve 6 people.

FOR THE BUTTERNUT CRÈME

1 butternut squash
2 tbsp olive oil
1 small (6-oz / 170-g) can tomato
    paste
splash of white wine
3 cups (750 ml) vegetable broth
a few sprigs of fresh sage
salt and freshly ground black pepper

FOR THE GOAT CHEESE CREAM

8 oz (200 g) cream cheese
⅔ cup (150 ml) soft, spreadable goat
    cheese (I use 1 small container
    of Cavour, but any soft goat
    cheese will do)

FOR GARNISH

5 tbsp (75 g) butter
a few nice sage leaves

Make the butternut crème: Peel the squash, cut it in half and remove the seeds, then dice it. Heat the oil in a heavy saucepan over high heat. Fry the squash briefly, then add the tomato paste and stir well, sauteing until it exudes a sweet aroma. Douse with the wine, stir for a few seconds, then add the broth. Add the sage sprigs and lower the heat to low just as the broth begins to boil. Let simmer for about 35 minutes with the lid askew.

Make the goat cheese cream: Blend the cheeses in a food processor to make a smooth sauce. Fill a pastry bag (if you have one) with the cream or cover the processor bowl. Refrigerate until use.

Puree the soup with an immersion blender until completely smooth (or let it cool a bit, then transfer it in batches to a standing blender to puree). Continue longer than you think is necessary, so it becomes a soft and silky crème.

Let the butternut crème cool to room temperature.

Make the garnish: Melt the butter in a saucepan over low heat. Carefully pour the clear part of the melted butter into a clean pan and discard the white solids at the bottom. Heat the clarified butter over medium-high heat and fry the sage leaves in it for a few seconds. Let them drain on a paper towel.

(Keep the clarified sage butter. You can use it to fry just about anything. Very good!)

Right before serving, fill small glasses with the butternut crème. Carefully pipe the goat cheese cream on top. If you don't have a pastry bag, you can use two spoons and flatten the cream with a knife.

Top with the fried sage and serve with a small spoon.

chickpea soup with sweet potato and feta crackers

2 leeks, white and light green parts, washed well and cut into rings
1 tsp butter
3 sweet potatoes, peeled and diced
3 sprigs fresh thyme
4½ cups (1 l) vegetable or chicken broth
1 (15-oz / 400-g) can chickpeas (if you don't wish to soak and cook dried chickpeas)
½ baguette
⅓ cup plus 2 tbsp (100 ml) crème fraîche
3½ oz (100 g) feta cheese
salt and freshly ground black pepper

In a large soup pot over medium heat, braise the leeks in the butter. Add the sweet potatoes and thyme and stir well. Stir in the broth and bring to a simmer; simmer for 30 minutes over low heat. Add the chickpeas, heat for 5 minutes, then use the back of a wooden spoon to smash the sweet potatoes against the sides of the pot to thicken the soup.

Preheat the broiler. Cut the baguette into slices and spread them with a bit of crème fraîche. Arrange the slices on a baking sheet, crumble the feta on top, and place them under the broiler to turn golden brown.

Taste the soup for salt and pepper and ladle into big bowls. Float a crostini on top and serve.

mushroom soup with spelt

1 oz (25 g) dried mushrooms, such
    as porcini
2 tbsp olive oil
1 onion, diced
2 stalks celery, sliced
1 carrot, peeled and diced
2 cloves garlic, minced
1 generous lb (500 g) fresh
    mushrooms, cleaned and
    chopped
½ cup (100 g) spelt (or barley)
2 tbsp tomato paste
splash of dry sherry
4½ cups (1 l) mushroom or
    vegetable broth
salt and freshly ground black pepper

Soak the dried mushrooms in a bowl of hot water for about
20 minutes.

Heat the oil in a large heavy saucepan over medium heat. Saute
the onion, celery, and carrot until the onion begins to color.

Add the garlic, stir briefly, then add the fresh mushrooms.
Saute, stirring frequently, for about 10 minutes, until the mushrooms release their moisture. Raise the heat and stir in the spelt.
Stir-fry, so the spelt can absorb the mushroom moisture, then
stir in the tomato paste. Once this gives off a sweet aroma, add
the sherry. Add the broth and the soaked mushrooms and their
liquid (strain the liquid if necessary to remove any grit). Season
the soup with salt and pepper and let simmer over low heat for
about 45 minutes, until the spelt is tender.

Serve with artisan bread.

crème of white beans & celeriac with chile oil

FOR THE SOUP
1½ cups (250 g) dried white beans
¼ cup olive oil
2 leeks, white and light green parts,
    washed well and finely chopped
½ celeriac, peeled and chopped
2 cloves garlic, minced
6½ cups (1.5 l) vegetable broth
2 tsp minced fresh rosemary, or 1 tsp
    dried rosemary
salt and freshly ground black pepper
juice of ½ lemon

FOR THE CHILE OIL
1 handful of dried chiles
2¼ cups (500 ml) grapeseed oil (or
    another light oil)

Make the soup: Soak the beans overnight in a bowl with
enough cold water to cover them generously.

Heat the oil in a large heavy saucepan and add the leeks and
celeriac. Saute, stirring constantly, until the leeks are soft. Add
the garlic, stir for a few seconds, then add the broth.

Drain the soaked beans and add them to the saucepan. Add
the rosemary and season with salt and pepper. Slowly bring to
a boil. Reduce the heat and let the soup simmer over low heat
with the lid askew for 1 hour.

In the meantime, make the chile oil: Put the chiles in a small
saucepan and add the oil. Gently heat the oil and let steep over
low heat for about 20 minutes.

Pour everything into a clean bottle. Let the oil cool completely,
then put the lid on the bottle. Keep the oil in a cool, dark place.

Over time the oil will turn more and more red, but you can use
it right away—it will be hot!

Puree the soup in batches in a blender and pour it back into
the saucepan, or use an immersion blender. You can also
choose to blend only half of the soup and leave it chunky—
that's nice too. Add the lemon juice and taste to see if the soup
needs more salt and pepper. Serve hot, trickling in a few drops
of spicy chile oil.

gentle soup of leeks & chestnuts

3 tbsp butter
9 oz (250 g) chestnuts, peeled (you
    can buy them peeled)
2 leeks, white and light green parts,
    washed well and sliced
10 oz (300 g) potatoes, peeled and
    diced
1 cup (250 ml) beer
about 4½ cups (1 l) chicken broth
salt and freshly ground black pepper
1 cup (250 ml) heavy cream

Melt the butter in a large saucepan over medium heat and
briefly saute the chestnuts, leeks, and potatoes. Add the beer,
let it evaporate for a few minutes, then add enough broth to
cover the vegetables by 1 inch (2.5 cm).

Let simmer over low heat until the potatoes are very tender,
15 to 20 minutes, then puree the soup until smooth with an immersion blender, or in batches in a standing blender.

Add water if needed, until the soup has the consistency you prefer. Taste for salt and pepper, then stir in half of the cream.

Serve with good bread and a swirl of the remaining cream.

irish potato soup

3 tbsp (50 g) butter
2 onions, diced
2 stalks celery, diced
1 clove garlic, minced or pressed
    with a garlic press
3 large potatoes, peeled and cubed
4½ cups (1 l) vegetable or chicken
    broth
salt and freshly ground black pepper
pinch of cayenne
1 bouquet garni: bay leaf, thyme, and
    parsley
1 cup plus 1 tbsp (250 g) crème
    fraîche

Melt the butter in a large saucepan and add the onions, celery, garlic, and potatoes. Cover the pan with the lid askew and saute the vegetables over low heat, stirring occasionally, for about 10 minutes, until soft. Add the broth, salt and pepper to taste, cayenne, and the bouquet garni. Let the soup simmer over low heat for about 1 hour.

Remove the bouquet garni and puree the soup with an immersion blender, or in batches in a standing blender, until silky and smooth.

Bring almost to a boil, then stir in the crème fraîche and heat gently for another 15 minutes.

Serve the soup garnished with a generous snipping of chives.

Co. Kerry, Ireland

split pea soup with squash and yogurt

1 butternut squash or sweet (pie)
    pumpkin
1 tbsp paprika (hot!)
1 tbsp fresh oregano
salt and freshly ground black pepper
2 to 3 tbsp olive oil
1 small onion, diced
1 tsp butter
½ cup (100 g) yellow split peas
¼ cup (50 g) green split peas
1 to 2 tbsp tomato paste
4½ cups (1 l) vegetable or chicken
    broth
1 small bunch fresh cilantro, chopped
½ cup (100 g) plain homemade
    yogurt (pages 28–29) or plain
    Greek yogurt

Preheat the oven to 350°F (180°C).

Peel the squash, cut it in half, and remove the pulp and seeds. Chop into 1-inch (2-cm) chunks and spread them out on a baking sheet. Sprinkle with the paprika, oregano, salt, and pepper, drizzle with the oil, and toss thoroughly. Spread out the chunks in a single layer.

Roast for about 30 minutes, until the edges begin to brown. Take them out and set aside until use.

Saute the onion in the butter in a saucepan over medium heat. Add the split peas and saute, stirring, for a minute. Stir in the tomato paste and saute until it exudes a sweet aroma—that's the sign that the sourness is gone. Stir in the broth and let the soup simmer for about 35 minutes over low heat.

Add the squash, heat through for a few minutes, then stir in the cilantro and taste for salt and pepper.

Ladle the soup into 4 nice bowls, scoop a dollop of yogurt on top, and garnish with cilantro. Serve, of course, with fresh crusty bread.

brousse cheese

In my book Home Made, I explained how easy it is to make cheese. This recipe is a small variation for a goat's and cow's milk cheese that's done in a snap.

You can make it an hour before your guests arrive, and isn't it nice to offer a fresh-made cheese?

1. **heat** 2¼ cups (500 ml) whole cow's milk, 2¼ cups (500 ml) goat's milk, 3 tbsp freshly squeezed lemon juice, and 2 tsp salt in a large saucepan over medium-high heat until the milk begins to curdle. Bring to a boil and boil for 3 minutes, until the clear whey has separated from the solid curd. 2. **line** a sieve with a clean cheesecloth, set it over a bowl, and pour in the mixture. Collect and save the liquid (the whey), as you can use it to make soda bread (page 23). 3. **squeeze** the curd in the cheese-cloth to remove as much whey as possible. 4. **press** the cloth with the fresh cheese into a *faiselle*, or a small container with a few holes. You can make this yourself from a can or plastic cup in which you poke some holes. Let the cheese firm in the fridge for at least 1 hour. Eat plain, or with honey for breakfast, or on a salad like the one on page 122.

warm chickpea salad with winter purslane, ginger, barley, brousse cheese, and nut oil dressing

You can replace the barley with couscous, bulgur, or wild rice.

FOR THE SALAD
¼ head green cabbage, thinly sliced
¼ cup (50 g) barley (preferably pearled)
½ cup (100 g) cooked chickpeas, or canned
1-inch (2-cm) piece fresh ginger, peeled and julienned
1 handful winter purslane, cleaned
1 cooked beet, peeled and cut into wedges
1¾ oz (50 g) brousse cheese (pages 120–121) or feta cheese

FOR THE DRESSING
1 small clove garlic, minced
3 tbsp plus 1 tsp (50 ml) red wine vinegar
salt and freshly ground black pepper
3 tbsp plus 1 tsp (50 ml) walnut or hazelnut oil
⅓ cup plus 2 tbsp (100 ml) light vegetable oil

Make the salad: Bring a large pot of water to a boil and add the cabbage; cook until al dente, about 10 minutes. Drain and set aside.

Cook the barley in a generous amount of boiling water until tender, about 15 minutes for pearled, or longer for hulled. Drain and set aside.

Make the dressing: Whisk all the ingredients together in a small bowl.

Pour 2 tbsp of the dressing into a wok over high heat. Add the cabbage and barley and stir-fry for a few minutes until the barley is hot and almost crisp. Add the chickpeas, ginger, purslane, and beet. Stir-fry briefly just to heat everything through. Spoon the salad onto a large platter. Pour the remaining dressing over it and crumble the cheese on top.

broiled brousse cheese with pickled pear

I like baked ricotta and I thought this would also work with brousse cheese. Fortunately it did—in fact, this cheese is a little tastier than ricotta. Eat with crusty bread, or with toasted brown soda bread (page 23).

FOR THE PICKLED PEARS
1 lb (500 g) firm-ripe pears
juice of 1 lemon
½ cup plus 2 tbsp (125 g) sugar
½ cup (125 ml) white wine vinegar
1-inch (2-cm) piece fresh ginger, peeled and grated
1 cinnamon stick
2 star anise
4 cloves
1 tbsp coriander seed

FOR THE CHEESE
1 brousse cheese (pages 120–121)
splash of olive oil
1 dried chile, ground in a mortar
1 tbsp coriander seed, ground in a mortar
1 tbsp fresh thyme leaves
pinch of flaky sea salt, such as Maldon

Make the pickled pears: Peel, quarter, and core the pears. Put the pears in a bowl and sprinkle with the lemon juice.

In a medium saucepan, bring the remaining ingredients gently to a boil, stirring until the sugar is dissolved. Add the pears, reduce the heat to low, and simmer for about 20 minutes, until the pears are tender but still hold their shape. Scoop them out of the pan and put them in a clean canning jar. Boil down the liquid until it's thickened slightly, then pour it into the jar. Screw the lid on and ideally let the pears pickle in the refrigerator for 1 month; you can also let them cool and continue right ahead.

Prepare the cheese: Preheat the broiler. Line a baking sheet with aluminum foil. Place the cheese on the foil and drizzle with the oil. Sprinkle with the chile, coriander, thyme, and salt. Place under the broiler and broil until the cheese begins to turn golden brown.

Serve the cheese warm with the pickled pears and a simple dark green salad, if you wish.

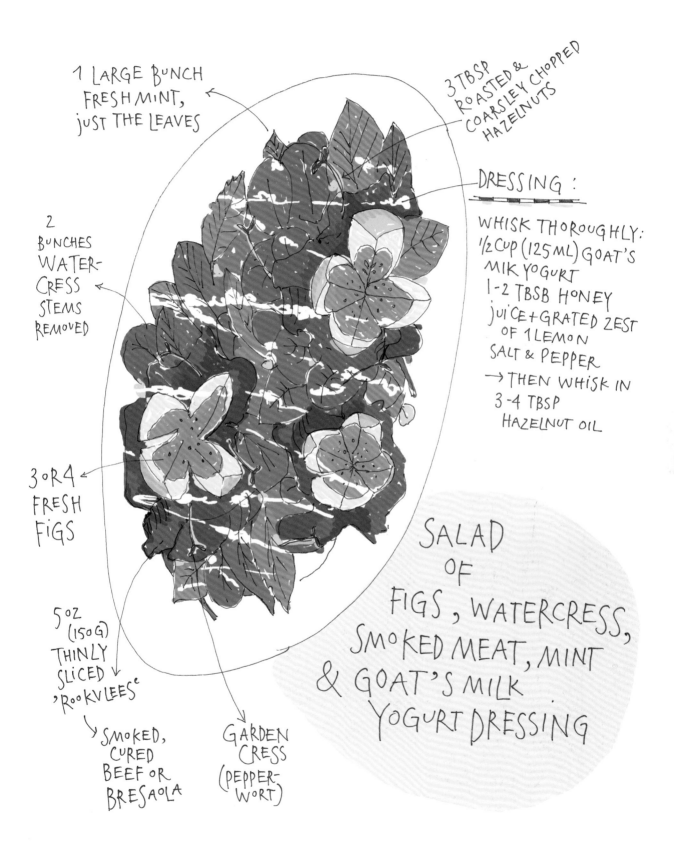

1 LARGE BUNCH
FRESH MINT,
JUST THE LEAVES

3 TBSP
ROASTED &
COARSLEY CHOPPED
HAZELNUTS

DRESSING :

WHISK THOROUGHLY:
1/2 CUP (125 ML) GOAT'S
MILK YOGURT
1-2 TBSB HONEY
JUICE + GRATED ZEST
OF 1 LEMON
SALT & PEPPER
→ THEN WHISK IN
3-4 TBSP
HAZELNUT OIL

2
BUNCHES
WATER-
CRESS
STEMS
REMOVED

3 OR 4
FRESH
FIGS

5 OZ
(150 G)
THINLY
SLICED
'ROOKVLEES'

↳ SMOKED,
CURED
BEEF OR
BRESAOLA

GARDEN
CRESS
(PEPPER-
WORT)

SALAD
OF
FIGS, WATERCRESS,
SMOKED MEAT, MINT
& GOAT'S MILK
YOGURT DRESSING

beet–marinated rainbow trout
with horseradish mousse, poppy seeds & apple

We put this on our menu in the restaurant for Christmas. It is so good that I'm giving you the recipe too.

FOR THE TROUT
2 cooked beets, peeled
2 tbsp fennel seed
1¼ cups (250 g) sea salt
2 cups (400 g) sugar
1 tbsp honey
2 rainbow trout fillets (about
    18 oz / 500 g), with skin (from
    1 large rainbow trout; ask your
    fishmonger to fillet it for you)

FOR THE HORSERADISH MOUSSE
5 to 6 tbsp (50 g) freshly grated
    horseradish, or 4 tbsp prepared
    horseradish
¼ cup (50 g) crème fraîche
salt and freshly ground black pepper
2 leaves gelatin, or 2 tsp unflavored
    gelatin powder
juice of ½ lemon
1 cup (250 ml) heavy cream
1 tsp poppy seeds

FOR THE DRESSING
1 small bunch fresh basil
pinch of salt
juice of ½ lemon
1 Granny Smith apple

Make the trout: Combine the beets, fennel seed, salt, sugar, and honey in a blender or food processor and blend until smooth. Pour a layer of the marinade into a shallow bowl. Put the trout fillets into the marinade. Pour the rest of the marinade on top. Cover the bowl and let the fish marinate in the refrigerator for 24 hours.

Make the horseradish mousse: Process the horseradish in a food processor until smooth, then add the crème fraîche and salt and pepper to taste and process to combine.

If using gelatin leaves, soak them in cold water until softened, then drain and squeeze out the excess water. Heat the lemon juice in a small saucepan over medium heat and add the gelatin (if using gelatin powder, sprinkle it in and stir gently until dissolved). Let the mixture cool briefly.

In a large bowl, whip the cream until stiff. Spoon 1 tbsp of the cream into the lemon-gelatin mixture and then whisk the mixture into the remaining cream, along with the horseradish mixture and poppy seeds. Scoop the mousse into 4 silicone baking cups and place them in the fridge to stiffen.

Just before serving, make the dressing: In a mortar, grind the basil leaves and salt. Stir in the lemon juice.

Take the fish fillets out of the marinade. Rinse and pat dry with paper towels. Using a thin, sharp knife, cut the fish into ultra-thin slices.

Cut the apple into ultra-thin slices as well. Place a few apple slices in the middle of each plate.

Invert the mousse cups on top of the apple. If you can't get the mousse out of the cups, you can dip the cups in warm water for 5 seconds (no longer!) and slide a sharp knife along the edges to loosen them. That should help.

Arrange the fish nicely on top of the horseradish mousse. Sprinkle some dressing on the side and serve with rye bread.

St. Stephens Green, Dublin

René the Organic Butcher, Nieuwmarkt, Amsterdam

potted ham

A simple starter, so make a lot at once. You can keep it in the fridge for up to a month, provided it's covered well with a layer of clarified butter.

FOR ABOUT 3 CUPS (700 ML)

3 onions, diced
½ cup plus 6 tbsp butter (200 g),
    divided
1 lb (500 g) good-quality cooked ham
½ tsp cayenne, or to taste
1 tsp curry powder
1 tsp paprika
salt and freshly ground black pepper
½ cup plus 2 tbsp (150 ml) apple
    cider or white wine

In a medium saucepan over low heat, saute the onions in 3 tbsp (50 g) of the butter until translucent but not browned. Put the onions and the ham in a food processor and grind coarsely.

Add the spices, process to combine, and taste for salt and pepper. The mixture can be seasoned strongly, as the flavors will be muted once it's chilled.

Put the mixture in a medium saucepan. Add the cider and let stew over low heat for 30 minutes, stirring occasionally.

Scoop the ham mixture into very clean, thick glass jars or glazed pottery. Tap the jars lightly on the counter to remove any air pockets. Let cool.

Gently melt the remaining ½ cup plus 3 tbsp (150 g) butter in a skillet. Slowly pour the clear part of the melted butter into a glass measuring cup and discard the white solids left in the pan. This is called clarifying butter.

Pour the clarified butter on top of the ham in the jars and let it set.

The potted ham will keep for weeks in the fridge; be sure to pour more clarified butter over the top to seal the surface each time you use some. Serve with toast and chutney, from the recipe below. The chutney on page 37 also goes nicely with this.

cranberry chutney with pear & ginger

Really delicious with the potted ham above, but also with all kinds of small game, pâté, or simply on a slice of bread or crostino with goat cheese.

FOR ABOUT 1½ LB (700 G)

⅓ cup (75 ml) cider vinegar
3 onions, peeled and diced
2 thumbs of grated fresh ginger
1 cinnamon stick
grated zest of ½ lemon
grated zest of 1 orange
1 small dried red chile
10 oz (300 g) fresh cranberries
¾ cup (125 g) raisins
2 pears, peeled, cored, and cubed
½ cup plus 2 tbsp (125 g) packed
    brown sugar
salt and freshly ground black pepper

In a medium saucepan over high heat, boil the vinegar, onion, ginger, cinnamon stick, lemon and orange zests, and chile for about 10 minutes. Add the cranberries, raisins, pears, and sugar. Reduce the heat and simmer for about half an hour.

Season to taste with salt and pepper.

Spoon into clean canning jars and refrigerate.

Ideally you want to make the chutney a day or two in advance, but you can also do it in the morning, as long as you have time to chill it.

The chutney will keep in the fridge for up to 2 weeks.

FRITTATA
OF KALE & BACON

5 OZ (150 G) BACON, CUBED

FRY IN O. OIL

FINELY CHOP A GENEROUS 1 LB (500 G) KALE & ADD TO THE PAN

ADD A SPLASH OF WHITE WINE, 1 BAY LEAF & SALT + PEPPER AND LET IT STEW OVER MEDIUM HEAT FOR 25 MIN. (MAYBE ADD SOME WATER)

BEAT 8 EGGS WITH 1/3 CUP + 2 TBSP (100 ML) HEAVY CREAM & PEPPER + SALT. ADD 1 CUP (100 G) GRATED PARMESAN CHEESE

SPOON THE KALE AND BACON INTO A 9-BY-13 INCH BAKING PAN LINED WITH PARCHMENT PAPER
THEN ADD THE EGG MIXTURE. ←

BAKE FOR 25 MINUTES AT 350°F (180°C) → LET IT COOL & CUT INTO SQUARES

Wicklow Mountains, Ireland

duck & sage terrine

Boo...!

You'll need some special equipment for this terrine: a meat grinder fitted with a die with medium-sized holes, or a good food processor.

FOR ABOUT 6 SERVINGS

1 lb (450 g) duck breast (2 breast
  halves)
⅓ cup (75 ml) milk
4 tsp sea salt
1 tsp freshly ground black pepper
1 tbsp finely chopped fresh sage
1 tsp fresh thyme leaves
½ tsp chopped fresh marjoram
¼ tsp allspice
¼ tsp ground ginger
2 tbsp tawny Port
1 tbsp Cognac, Armagnac, or other
  brandy
½ cup (125 ml) crème fraîche
1 egg, beaten
3 tbsp shelled pistachios
½ cup plus 2 tbsp (150 g) butter
a few fresh sage leaves

YEAH!

Pull the fat off of the duck breasts with your fingers or use a sharp knife. Wrap the fat in plastic wrap and place in the freezer until firm but not frozen, about 1 hour.

In a meat grinder or food processor, grind the duck breast meat to medium, then grind the chilled fat. Add all the remaining ingredients except the butter and sage and grind everything into a nice smooth mixture.

Scoop the duck mixture into an ovenproof dish and cover it with aluminum foil. Place the terrine in the fridge to let the flavors develop for 4 hours or overnight.

Preheat the oven to 250°F (125°C). Bake the terrine for about 2 hours, depending on the size of your terrine dish, covered with the foil for the first 1½ hours, then uncovered, until firm and nicely browned on top.

Carefully take the terrine out of the oven. Beware: The meat will have shrunk and the grease surrounding it is liquid. Let cool.

Melt the butter in a saucepan over low heat. Pour the clear part of the melted butter into a glass measuring cup and discard the white solids left in the pan.

Heat the clear butter in a clean saucepan and briefly fry the sage leaves in it. Let them drain on a paper towel. Use the sage leaves to garnish the terrine, and pour the clarified sage butter over the terrine. Let the butter set and refrigerate the terrine until ready to use.

Serve the terrine at room temperature with toast.

Glendalough

Paris

& Chris

beet blinis with salmon marinated in star anise syrup

This recipe is for 25 pieces or more. You can freeze both the blinis and salmon when there are leftovers, so make a lot. I find them truly spectacular.

FOR THE SALMON

1 tbsp freshly ground black pepper

2 tbsp salt

½ cup plus 1 tbsp (200 g) honey

6 star anise

2 tbsp soy sauce

2 tbsp white wine vinegar

14 to 18 oz (400 to 500 g) smoked
   salmon fillet with skin

FOR THE BLINIS

1 (¼-oz / 7-g) envelope active dry
   yeast

1 tsp sugar

1 small cooked beet, peeled

1 cup (125 g) all-purpose flour

½ cup (125 ml) milk

pinch of salt

2 eggs

2 tbsp (25 g) butter, melted, plus
   1 tsp for the pan

AND FURTHER

½ cup (100 g) mascarpone

3 tbsp pomegranate seeds

First marinate the salmon: This should be done at least 1 day and ideally 2 days in advance.

In a small saucepan over high heat, bring ½ cup (125 ml) water, the pepper, salt, honey, and star anise to a boil. Reduce the heat to low and simmer for about 15 minutes. Let cool, then stir in the soy sauce and vinegar. Pour the marinade into a bowl and add the salmon. Press so that the salmon is well covered. Cover the bowl and let the fish marinate in the fridge for at least 24 hours.

The next day, make the blini batter: Combine the yeast and sugar with 3 tbsp (50 ml) warm water and set aside for a few minutes. Chop the beet and collect 1 to 2 tbsp of the pink liquid. Set the liquid aside. Puree the beet in a food processor, add the flour, and process to combine.

Heat the milk to lukewarm, then pour it into the yeast mixture. Turn on the food processor again and pour the milk mixture through the feed tube into the beet mixture. Add the salt, eggs, and melted butter. Set aside for at least 1 hour in a warm place to rise.

Whisk the pink liquid from the beets into the mascarpone and refrigerate until ready to use.

Just before serving: Rinse the marinade from the salmon. Pat it completely dry and use a long thin knife to slice it diagonally into thin slices. Heat a nonstick saute pan over medium heat. Melt 1 tsp butter in the pan and spoon about 2 tbsp blini batter into the pan. Fry about 4 blinis at a time. Flip them with two forks when the holes form on top. Let drain on paper towels. Cover with a swirl of salmon, spread with a bit of pink mascarpone, and sprinkle with the pomegranate seeds.

watercress with smoked almond
goat cheese scoops & grapes in red wine syrup

An awfully simple recipe that looks very flashy. Instead of the grapes you could use fresh cranberries or quartered fresh figs.

If you can't find smoked almonds, you can use regular almonds.

½ of a 750-ml bottle red wine
½ cup plus 2 tbsp (125 g) turbinado
    or Demerara sugar
3 star anise
8 cardamom pods
5 oz (150 g) seedless red grapes
salt and freshly ground black pepper
7 oz (200 g) soft goat cheese
⅓ cup (50 g) smoked almonds
1 bunch fresh watercress, stems
    removed

Heat the wine in a medium saucepan over medium-high heat. Add the sugar and stir to dissolve, then add the anise and cardamom and bring to a boil. Boil the syrup for about 25 minutes, until it's slightly thicker. Reduce the heat to low and add the grapes. Warm the grapes in the syrup for about 7 minutes.

Remove the pan from the heat and let the syrup cool. Taste and add salt and pepper if needed.

Divide the goat cheese into 12 equal portions. With clean hands, roll the portions into small balls.

Pulse the almonds in a food processor until coarsely ground. Roll the goat cheese balls in the almonds to coat them.

Place the cheese balls on a tray or baking sheet, cover them, and place them in the fridge for 1 hour to firm up.

To serve, wash and dry the watercress. Arrange some nice leaves over 4 plates. Arrange the goat cheese balls on top and spoon grapes in syrup around the cheese.

Docklands, Dublin

MAIN COURSES

Paris

THIS RIDICULOUSLY DELICIOUS MEAL TAKES TIME, BUT NO EFFORT

PULLED PORK

→ 1 PIECE BONELESS PORK SHOULDER ABOUT 3¼ LB (1,5 KG)

→ SMOKER (YOU CAN EASILY MAKE THIS YOURSELF SEE MY BOOK 'HOME MADE')

→ AT LEAST 6 TBSP WOOD CHIPS. (YOU CAN ADD OTHER THINGS, SEE 'HOME MADE'

PREHEAT YOUR OVEN TO JUST UNDER 300°F (140°C)
RUB YOUR MEAT WITH MEAT RUB FOR EXAMPLE THIS ONE

THE NIGHT BEFORE IS EVEN BETTER OF COURSE

2 TABLESPOONS OF EACH:

· GOOD PAPRIKA, CHILE FLAKES, BROWN SUGAR & A LITTLE LESS SALT

PLACE THE MEAT ON TOP OF A RACK IN THE SMOKER, COVER AND PLACE THE STOVE OVER LOW HEAT UNTIL IT BEGINS SMOKING.
THEN PLACE THE ENTIRE SMOKING THING IN THE OVEN.
DO SOMETHING ELSE ....

♪ la di da ♫

THE MEAT IS DONE AFTER ABOUT 5 HOURS. (DO YOU HAVE A MEAT THERMOMETER?)
→ THE INTERNAL TEMPERATURE SHOULD BE 175°F (80°C)
PULL THE MEAT WITH 2 FORKS.
EAT ON A ROLL, WITH A LICK OF MUSTARD.
→ OR CHECK THE NEXT PAGE FOR MORE GOOD TIPS...

doubles: miraculous rolls for pulled pork

A few years ago a friend gave me a book, Madhur Jaffrey's World Vegetarian, *not only because it's a great book, but most of all because it has a recipe for "Doubles"—a recipe that has become one of our favorites too. Mrs. Jaffrey got her recipe from Trinidad, where they serve the rolls with fried shark. For her book she made it into a vegetarian recipe, with chickpeas and tomatoes. Delicious! I now introduce it with pulled pork. Eat it with any or all of the side dishes on the next three pages—it's all good. The most important tip I can give you is: Make plenty!*

3½ cups (450 g) self-rising flour
pinch of salt
½ tsp ground turmeric
about 4½ cups (1 l) sunflower oil
    for frying

Sift the flour, salt, and turmeric into a large bowl. Add about 1¼ cups (300 ml) water and knead into a smooth ball of soft dough. Use more or less water as necessary. Cover the bowl and let rest for 1 hour.

Divide the dough into 16 equal parts and roll each into a ball with your hands. One by one, roll the balls out on a lightly floured surface into flat rounds the size of a CD. Cover with plastic wrap until ready to use.

Heat 1½ to 2 inches (4 to 5 cm) oil in a deep saucepan over medium-high heat. When it begins to smoke, slide 1 dough round carefully onto the bottom. In no time the round will begin to puff up like a balloon; let it fry for 10 seconds, then flip it with a skimmer.

Drain on paper towels. Continue frying the rest of the rounds. If the dough rounds have shrunk as they rested, simply roll them out again.

Slice the doubles open like a pita bread and fill with meat and vegetables.

sauerkraut salad with hazelnuts

2¼ lb (1 kg) prepared sauerkraut
⅓ cup (75 ml) cider vinegar or
    sherry vinegar
2 to 3 tbsp ginger syrup from a jar of
    preserved ginger
½ cup plus 2 tbsp (150 ml)
    hazelnut oil
salt and freshly ground black
    pepper
⅔ cup (75 g) hazelnuts

Place the sauerkraut in a sieve and rinse it under the faucet. Let drain. For the dressing, whisk the vinegar and ginger syrup thoroughly and whisk in the hazelnut oil in a thin stream. Taste and season with salt and pepper.

Toast the nuts in a dry skillet until they color slightly. Chop them coarsely.

Mix everything together and serve with rich meat: pulled pork, for example, or small game.

dark sweet–tart apple syrup

This goes so well with rich, fatty meat like fried pork chops or sausage.

3 apples (a crisp, sweet, and slightly
    tart apple such as Granny Smith)
2 shallots
2 tbsp butter
1 tbsp fresh thyme leaves
⅓ cup (75 ml) balsamic vinegar
3 tbsp golden syrup or brown sugar
salt and freshly ground black pepper

Peel, core, and dice the apples. Peel and dice the shallots. Melt the butter in a medium saucepan over medium heat and add the apples, shallots, and thyme; saute for about 7 minutes, stirring occasionally, until the apples are tender. Add the vinegar, stir in the syrup, and season with salt and pepper. If the sauce is too thick, add some water.

Eat warm or cold.

fried parsnips

2¼ lb (1 kg) parsnips
coarse salt and freshly ground black
    pepper
1 tbsp fresh thyme leaves
drizzle of olive oil

Preheat the oven to 350°F (180°C).

Peel the parsnips and quarter them lengthwise. Spread them out on a baking sheet. Sprinkle with the salt, pepper, and thyme. Drizzle with some oil and toss to coat. Bake for about 20 minutes, depending on their size, until tender. The tips will become very dark, but that's good.

white beans in tomato sauce

Yes, I'm actually giving you a recipe for it. Try it yourself . . . isn't it delicious?

1¾ cups (300 g) dried white beans
salt
2 tbsp olive oil
1 onion, diced
1 clove garlic, pressed in a garlic press
2 (28-oz / 800-g) cans peeled whole
    tomatoes
1 tbsp Worcestershire sauce
1 tbsp brown sugar
1 tbsp prepared hot mustard
freshly ground black pepper

Put the beans in a large bowl, add water to cover by several inches and let soak for 12 hours.

Drain the beans in a colander, rinse them well, then put them in a large saucepan and cover generously with water. Boil over medium heat until just about tender, 1 to 1½ hours (they will cook some more later in the sauce). Taste and add some salt halfway through. Drain and set aside.

Heat the oil in a heavy skillet over medium heat and saute the onion and garlic for 3 minutes. Drain the tomatoes, chop them, and add them to the onion. Add the Worcestershire sauce, brown sugar, and mustard. Reduce the heat to low and stir in the beans.

Let everything simmer for 30 minutes. Season with salt and pepper.

Eat with pulled pork, or on toast or with sausage.

hot relish

1 large onion, diced
6 fresh hot red chiles, chopped
¼ cup vinegar
3 tbsp sugar
salt

Chop the onion and chiles fine in a food processor. Heat the vinegar and sugar in a small saucepan. Add the chile mixture and cook for no longer than 3 minutes. If necessary, add 2 tbsp of water to loosen the mixture. Season with salt.

Spoon the sauce into a small bowl and serve with pulled pork, or spread on a croque monsieur. The relish will keep in a clean jar in the fridge for a few weeks.

PIZZA BIANCA
TO WHICH I TIP MY HAT

BASIC RECIPE
FOR PIZZA
DOUGH
(FACING PAGE)

SAUTÉ 2 ONIONS
IN BUTTER
OVER LOW HEAT.
THEY SHOULD
BE SOFT
BUT NOT
BROWN.
SEASON WITH
SALT & PEPPER
AND ARRANGE
OVER PIZZA
CRUST.

LAYER ON
A FEW
SLICES
OF GOOD
PROSCIUTTO

1 BALL OF
FRESH
MOZZARELLA
SLICED.

2-3
RIPE
FIGS
HALVED

DRIZZLE
SOME
GOOD OLIVE
OIL
OVER IT,
RIGHT BEFORE
SERVING

pizza: oof's basic recipe

You may not expect this, but Oof, not me, is the one who makes the pizza at home. When he makes them the crusts are nicely crisp and very thin. So good. It actually doesn't matter what he puts on them, they are always heavenly. The secret is not to add too many toppings: The crust will become soggy, and we wouldn't want that. A preheated pizza stone in the oven helps enormously. Instead of a pizza stone we use twice-baked kitchen tiles, which you might even have lying around. They fit nicely on a baking sheet and the effect is the same. This recipe makes enough dough for pizza for 4. We like to make smaller ones (like the one in the picture), so you'll probably be able to make 6 to 8 of those smaller ones with this recipe.

1 (¼-oz / 7-g) envelope active dry
    yeast
3¼ cups (400 g) all-purpose flour
¾ cup (100 g) semolina flour
pinch of salt

Dissolve the yeast in ¼ cup (60 ml) lukewarm water in a bowl. Stir in another 1 cup (240 ml) lukewarm water and both flours. Add the salt and knead into a dough. Take the dough out of the bowl, dust the counter with flour, and keep kneading the dough for at least 10 minutes, until it's nice and smooth. Put it back in the bowl, cover it with plastic wrap, and let it rest in a draft-free place for 1½ hours.

Place your pizza stone in the oven and preheat the oven to a very high temperature: 450°F (240°C) if possible.

Knead your dough once more for a few minutes, divide it into a few equal portions, and let them rest on the counter for about half an hour. Roll them out one at a time on a well-floured surface.

Choose your own toppings.

A FEW TBSP THICK TOMATO SAUCE, SPINATA ROMANA (THAT'S A SALAMI), FETA, AND JALAPEÑO PEPPERS

PIZZA BIANCA:
SAUTEED ONIONS, SLICED BAKED POTATO, BRIEFLY FRIED PORCINI, AND TALEGGIO (A MOUNTAIN CHEESE)

tartiflette with cod

I also could have called this recipe "fish pie," but I didn't. I love fish pie, but I also love tartiflette, which is almost the same, but is very French and made with bacon instead of fish and with lots and lots of Reblochon, a delicious French cheese from the Alps. If you've ever been skiing there, you probably know the meal.

I have combined the two and swapped the Reblochon for Comté, another favorite of mine. The result is ridiculously good. You need only a spoon, a blanket on the couch, and a good movie. Delicious!

8 firm potatoes, peeled
3 white onions, peeled
butter for greasing
salt and freshly ground black pepper
2 tbsp fresh thyme leaves
9 oz (250 g) Comté, grated
9 oz (250 g) cod fillets, in squares
about 1¼ cups (300 ml) heavy cream
pinch of paprika

Preheat the oven to 350°F (180°C). Slice the potatoes as thinly as possible, preferably with a mandoline. Do the same with the onions.

Butter an oven dish.

Make layers: Start with the potato, then onions, salt and pepper, thyme, some cheese, some fish; continue until you've used all (trying to end with potato and reserving some cheese and thyme for the top).

Season the cream with salt and pepper. Pour it over the dish and sprinkle some cheese, thyme, and the paprika on top.

Cover the dish with aluminum foil and place on a baking sheet in case it leaks.

Bake the tartiflette for 20 minutes. Remove the foil and bake for another 15 minutes, until golden brown and bubbly.

Of course you don't have to use cod. You can use a different fish, meat, or vegetable instead.

+ fresh salmon

+ bacon

+ smoked trout

+ even chunks of smoked chicken

+ 2 handfuls of small shrimp

+ It's also nice to pull 2 pieces of duck confit and arrange pieces among the potatoes.

+ some blanched wild spinach, or slices of blanched green cabbage

+ You could also cut 1 head radicchio into thick slices, sear them in a grill pan, and arrange those between the potato and cheese.

Howth, Ireland

baked risotto with cauliflower, gruyère & crisp bread crumbs

Hardly any work and done in a snap. Eat with just a spoon while watching a good movie.

1 small head cauliflower, cut into
  florets
1 tbsp olive oil
2 small onions, diced
1 clove garlic, sliced
7 oz (200 g) Arborio rice
½ cup (125 ml) white wine
2¼ cups (500 ml) chicken or
  vegetable broth
7 oz (200 g) Gruyère, grated
2 or 3 slices dry white bread

Boil the cauliflower in water for 10 minutes, until al dente. Drain.

Preheat the oven to 350°F (180°C).

Heat the oil in a cast-iron skillet. Add the onion and saute for about 5 minutes, add the garlic and cook for 1 minute, then add the rice. Saute all of this for another 2 minutes or so. Add the wine and then pour in the broth. Bring to a boil. Stir in the cauliflower and cheese. Put a lid on the skillet.

Put the skillet in the oven and bake the risotto for 25 minutes, or until all the liquid is absorbed.

Grind the dry bread in a food processor or mince with a knife.

Uncover the skillet about 5 minutes before the risotto is done (Watch out! Hot!) and sprinkle the bread crumbs on top.

Bake, uncovered, until browned, then serve.

All these fondues are for 6 people as a snack or apéritif, for 4 people as starter, or for 2 people as a main course.

cheese fondue from stilton, cream cheese & *belegen* (aged) gouda

¾ cup (200 ml) dry white wine
  (reserve a few spoonfuls)
7 oz (200 g) cream cheese (I use
  Philadelphia)
3½ oz (100 g) Stilton, crumbled
7 oz (200 g) aged Gouda, grated
1 tbsp cornstarch
salt and freshly ground black pepper

In a heavy skillet, heat the wine almost to a boil. Lower the heat, add the cheeses, and let them melt, stirring constantly. The mixture shouldn't boil. Mix the reserved wine with the cornstarch and stir it into the cheese. Stir well.

Season the fondue with salt and pepper.

Eat with endive leaves and pear and some crusty bread if you wish.

port salut fondue with salted thyme cookies

FOR THE THYME COOKIES
¾ cup (100 g) all-purpose flour
3 tbsp (50 g) butter
1 tsp salt
1 tbsp fresh thyme leaves

FOR THE FONDUE
½ cup (100 g) crème fraîche
¾ cup (200 ml) white Port
1 tbsp all-purpose flour
7 oz (200 g) port salut, in small
  chunks
7 oz (200 g) Emmenthaler, in small
  chunks
salt and freshly ground black pepper

Make the thyme cookies: In a bowl, combine all the ingredients into a dough, adding a few drops of ice water to make it smooth. Wrap the dough in plastic wrap and refrigerate for 30 minutes.

Preheat the oven to 350°F (180°C).

On a well-floured surface, roll out the dough ¼ inch (6 mm) thick. Cut out cookies and place them on a greased baking sheet.

Scrape the leftover dough together and repeat until finished. Bake about 25 minutes, until crisp and golden brown. Let them cool on a rack.

Make the fondue: Blend the crème fraîche, Port, and flour into a paste. Place the paste in a saucepan over medium heat. Add the cheeses and let them melt. Stir until the mixture is smooth and season with salt and pepper. Eat with the thyme cookies.

mushroom fondue with roquefort & brie

2 tbsp (25 g) butter
1 onion, diced
9 oz (250 g) wild mushrooms,
  chopped
1 tbsp fresh thyme leaves
salt and freshly ground pepper
1½ tbsp all-purpose flour
1 cup (250 ml) dry white wine
18 oz (500 g) brie
5½ oz (150 g) Roquefort, crumbled

Heat the butter in a heavy skillet over medium heat. Saute the onion and mushrooms and sprinkle in the thyme, salt, and pepper. Sprinkle in the flour and cook briefly.

Douse with white wine and heat to a simmer.

Cut the rind from the brie and cut the cheese into smaller chunks.

Melt the cheeses in the pan, stirring until you have a nice smooth fondue. Serve with the pear, toasted bread, and celery sticks.

thinly sliced veal

2 tbsp chopped fresh sage
1 clove garlic, minced
2 tbsp finely grated lemon zest
2 tbsp fennel seed
2 tbsp ground coriander
2 tbsp cracked white peppercorns
2 tbsp coarse sea salt
2¼ lb (1 kg) veal loin
generous splash of olive oil
½ of a (750-ml) bottle white wine

Mix the sage, garlic, lemon zest, and spices in a mortar and coarsely grind. Spread a sheet of plastic wrap on the counter and sprinkle it with half of the mixture. Place the veal loin on top and sprinkle it with the remaining spice mixture to cover the veal completely. Set aside in the refrigerator for 1 hour, or ideally overnight.

Let the meat come to room temperature before you bake it. Unwrap the meat but don't touch the spices.

Preheat the oven to 350°F (170°C).

Heat some oil in an ovenproof saute pan and sear the meat on both sides, flipping it continuously.

Add the wine and place the pan in the oven. Bake for 45 to 50 minutes, or until the internal temperature is 150°F (65°C) for medium-rare. Turn the meat halfway through and baste it a few times with the cooking liquid, to prevent it from becoming too dry.

Let the meat rest under aluminum foil for 15 minutes before slicing it into the thinnest possible slices.

Serve with the red onion & pomegranate compote below, as well as mashed potato and a salad or the cauliflower risotto on page 152.

red onion & pomegranate compote

8 red onions, sliced into thin rings
½ cup (100 g) packed brown sugar
⅓ cup plus 2 tbsp (100 ml) red wine vinegar
⅓ cup plus 2 tbsp (100 ml) red wine
generous splash of grenadine syrup
3 to 4 tbsp pomegranate seeds

Place the onions, sugar, and vinegar in a saucepan and slowly bring it to a boil. Simmer for about 10 minutes, until the onions are soft and the liquid becomes sticky. Add the wine and simmer for another 10 minutes. Let cool a little.

Add the grenadine syrup and stir in the pomegranate seeds. Let the compote cool completely and spoon it into 2 or 3 clean jars. Keep in the refrigerator for up to several weeks.

Howth, Co. Dublin

Wicklow Mountains

soup with lentils, lemon, cilantro & feta

There actually isn't a moment in the day when this soup doesn't go well. That's why I put it among the main courses. This recipe is for 2 generous main course portions, but if you eat it as a starter it will serve 4 (in which case add a little more broth).

2 tbsp olive oil
1 onion, minced
1 cup (200 g) yellow split peas
½ celeriac, cleaned and cubed
2 tsp cumin
2 tsp coriander
pinch of cayenne
1 small clove garlic, minced
salt and freshly ground black pepper
4½ cups (1 l) vegetable broth
zest and juice of 1 lemon
a few sprigs fresh cilantro
2 to 3 tbsp crumbled feta cheese

Heat the oil in a medium saucepan over medium-high heat. Add the onion and saute for 5 minutes, until translucent. Add the lentils and celeriac. Stir-fry them briefly, then add the spices and garlic. Season with salt and pepper.

Stir in the broth and lower the heat. Let the soup simmer for about 20 minutes, or until lentils are nicely al dente.

Just before serving, add the lemon zest and juice to the soup. Chop the cilantro and add it to the soup.

Ladle the soup into big bowls and crumble some feta on top.

Serve with artisan bread.

BEAN COCOTTE
WITH ROASTED GARLIC

PLACE IN A SMALL
OVEN DISH
4 CLOVES GARLIC
1 TBSP OLIVE OIL
ROAST IN THE OVEN
AT 350° F (180°C)
UNTIL GOLDEN BROWN
& SOFT (ABT. 40 MIN)
LEAVE THE OVEN ON.

OR MORE
IF YOU
WISH ←

THEN: PUT OUT 4 COCOTTES (SINGLE SERVING OVENPROOF
DISHES) ON THE COUNTER. DEVIDE BETWEEN THEM:

1 CUP (250G)
COOKED WHITE
BEANS

1 CARROT,
SLICED

4 STALKS
CELERY,
SLICED

2 (14½ OZ) CANS
DICED TOMATOES
DRAINED

1 TBSP FRESH
THYME LEAVES

+

1 TBSP
MINCED
FRESH ROSEMARY

+

SALT
&
PEPPER

PRESS A ROASTED GARLIC CLOVE TROUGH A GARLIC PRESS
ONTO EACH OF THE COCOTTES. SPRINKLE ALL WITH
BREAD CRUMBS (FROM 2 SLICES OF BREAD) & GRATED GRUYÈRE-
CHEESE TO TASTE

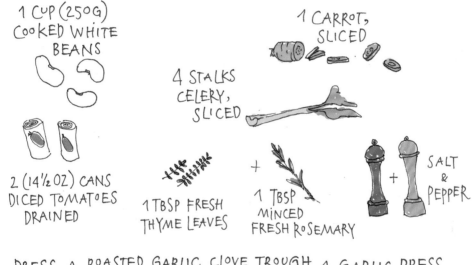

GENEROUSLY DRIZZLE WITH OLIVE OIL
PLACE THEM ON A BAKING SHEET (IN CASE OF LEAKS)
BAKE UNTIL TENDER, ABOUT 35 MIN. EAT WITH 1
SPOON →

mashed potatoes with brussels sprouts, orange & smoked sausage

No winter without mashed potatoes. Don't you agree?

3 lb (1.5 kg) potatoes, peeled
½ pound (250 g) smoked pork
    sausage, such as kielbasa
2 lb (1 kg) Brussels sprouts, cleaned
about ½ cup (125 ml) chicken broth
3 tbsp (50 g) butter
zest and juice of 1 orange
salt and freshly ground black pepper

Boil the potatoes and the sausage in its casing until the potatoes are cooked through. Drain and set aside.

In the meantime, boil the Brussels sprouts for 10 minutes, until al dente. Drain. Cut the sausage into slices. Heat the broth in a small saucepan. Mash the potatoes with a little hot broth and the butter. Spoon in the Brussels sprouts and season with orange zest, a little orange juice, salt, and pepper.

Serve, garnished with the sliced sausage, with mustard on the side.

sweet potato mash with green cabbage & parsnips

½ head green cabbage, thinly sliced
salt
3 lb (1.5 kg) sweet potatoes, cleaned
    and chopped
2 parsnips
3 tbsp olive oil
1 clove garlic, pressed through a
    garlic press
salt and freshly ground black pepper
7 tbsp (100 g) butter
splash of milk
2 tbsp fresh thyme leaves

Preheat the oven to 350°F (180°C).

Boil the cabbage in salted water until it is al dente. In a different pan, boil the sweet potatoes in salted water until tender. Drain.

Peel the parsnips and cut lengthwise into long equal pieces. Spread them out on a baking sheet and coat with the oil, garlic, salt, and pepper. Bake 15 to 20 minutes, until tender, then cut them into smaller chunks of about 1 inch (3 cm).

Mash the sweet potatoes, stirring in butter and milk until you have a nice smooth puree.

Season with thyme, salt, and pepper.

Stir in the cabbage strips and the roasted parsnip.

Serve alone or with a meat stew.

Marie at the Nieuwmarkt, Amsterdam

whole organic chicken stuffed with pork, veal & sage sausage

FOR THE STUFFING

2 large onions, diced

3 tbsp (50 g) butter

1 small bunch of fresh sage, finely chopped

1 lb (500 g) ground veal

8¾ oz (250 g) pork sausage, casings removed

1 egg white

½ tsp salt

freshly ground black pepper

AND FURTHER

1 organic chicken

3 tbsp (50 g) butter, at room temperature

salt and freshly ground black pepper

⅓ cup plus 2 tbsp (100 ml) marsala wine

Make the stuffing: Saute the onions in the butter in a heavy pan over low heat until they are soft and sweet. Add the sage. Let cool a little while you debone the chicken. Deboning a chicken sounds more complicated than it actually is. You only need a pair of kitchen scissors, a sharp knife, and some nerve.

Begin by cutting the chicken along its spine. Cut along the bone from head to tail.

Then carve the skin and the flesh away from the ribs. You want to follow the skeleton with short, sharp strokes of the knife. When you reach the legs and wings, you'll need to break or cut the bone to separate the legs and wings from the rib section. Leave the leg bones and the wing bones intact.

Ply your fingers between breast and breast bone and carefully pull the flesh off. Discard the skeleton.

Place the boned chicken in front of you, skin side down. Spread it out and flatten the flesh.

In a large bowl, combine the onion mixture with all the remaining ingredients for the stuffing, and use your hands to knead it into a smooth mixture. Knead well until it becomes slightly sticky, and shape it into a nice ball. Place the ball on the spread-out chicken and pull the skin up, so that you'll end up with a nicely filled whole chicken. Fasten the two halves together with the skewers. Because the skin of a good chicken is strong, it will stay together.

Flip the bird over, seam side down, and spread it with the soft butter. Season with salt and pepper.

Preheat the oven to 350°F (180°C). Put the chicken in a roasting pan and bake about 1 hour, until the juices around the transition from legs to breast are clear and the meat feels firm. The internal temperature should be 150°F (65°C).

Remove the chicken from the roasting pan and let it rest under aluminum foil for 10 minutes. Strain the roasting liquid into a saucepan and bring it to a boil. Add the marsala and whisk it into a smooth sauce. Serve with the chicken.

FLUFFY PIE WITH STILTON &
POACHED PEAR

FLUFFY PIE WITH CRUMBLED GOAT CHEESE,
ARTICHOKES & BLANCHED SPINACH

fluffy pies

Recently I wondered why hearty pies from France always are so nicely fluffy and creamy. The simple answer came from the French Sophie, who cooks in our restaurant: "Less egg, more cream," she said. And it's true.

FOR THE DOUGH
2½ cups (300 g) all-purpose flour
salt
½ cup plus 2 tbsp (150 g) butter,
    plus extra for greasing
1 egg yolk
4 to 5 tablespoons ice water

FOR THE FILLING
2 eggs
1 cup (250 ml) crème fraîche
salt and freshly ground black pepper
freshly grated nutmeg
whatever else you want to put in it
    (see above)

Make the dough: Combine the flour and salt in a large bowl and cut in the butter until the mixture resembles a coarse meal. Add the yolk and enough ice water to make a soft ball. Pat the dough into a flat slab and wrap it in plastic wrap. Refrigerate for 30 minutes, or ideally 1 hour.

Butter a 9½-inch (24-cm) springform pan.

Take the dough out of the fridge and let it come to room temperature, about 15 minutes.

Dust the counter and rolling pin with flour and roll out the dough until it's ¼ inch (.5 cm) thick. Roll the dough back over the rolling pin and arrange it in the pan. With your thumb, push the dough against the sides of the pan. Cut off the edges with a knife.

Preheat the oven to 350°F (180°C).

Make the filling: In a medium bowl, beat the eggs with the crème fraîche and add salt, pepper, and nutmeg.

Place a filling of choice on the dough and pour the crème fraîche mixture on top.

Bake the pie for about 25 minutes, until the cream filling is set but still jiggles in the center. It will firm up as it cools.

THOSE HEARTY FRENCH PIES
THAT I LOVE

TAKE, FOR EXAMPLE, QUICHE LORRAINE

PER PIE, FOR 4 TO 6 PEOPLE, SPRINKLE
1½ CUPS (150 G) GRATED GRUYÈRE
ONTO THE DOUGH IN THE
SPRINGFORM PAN &
CONTINUE AS DESCRIBED
IN THE RECIPE OPPOSITE

COVER THE PIE WITH
(1, 4, OR 6) SLICES OF
RAW BACON

duck breast with pink raisins & apricots

This is one of those handy recipes for when you expect many guests. You can prepare the sauce and puree in advance, and you'll only have to heat it before you serve dinner. The duck breast will be done in a snap. You'll let it rest under aluminum foil while you eat your starters and only then will you cut the meat.

⅔ cup (100 g) yellow raisins
3½ oz (100 g) dried apricots
1 small cooked beet, peeled and
     cubed
½ cup plus 2 tbsp (150 ml) ruby Port
4 duck breasts
salt and freshly ground black pepper
2 to 3 tbsp raspberry vinegar
1 tbsp fennel seed
1 tbsp prepared mustard
7 tbsp (100 g) cold butter, cut into
     chunks, plus more for the pan

Combine the dried fruits, the beet, and the Port and let them sit overnight.

Score a diamond pattern in the skin of the duck breasts and sprinkle both sides with salt and pepper.

Let the meat come to room temperature.

Drain the dried fruits, reserving the liquid and discarding the beet. Strain the marinade into a saucepan.

Heat the marinade with the raspberry vinegar, ⅓ cup (75 ml) water, and the fennel seeds over medium-high heat. Add the dried fruits. Bring to a boil and cook about 10 minutes, until the liquid is reduced. Lower the heat, stir in the mustard, and then add the butter a little at a time. Make sure the sauce doesn't boil, and stir until it thickens a bit.

Meanwhile, melt some butter over high heat in a saute pan and add the duck breasts, skin side down. Cook them for 10 minutes on the skin side, then another 5 minutes on the other side.

Let the meat rest for 10 minutes under aluminum foil on a cutting board, then slice it.

Serve dressed with the dried-fruit sauce, with celeriac puree (below) and green vegetables on the side.

celeriac puree with thyme

2 small celeriacs or 1 big one, peeled
     and cubed
2 bay leaves
½ cup (125 ml) crème fraîche
2 tbsp fresh thyme leaves
salt and freshly ground black pepper
freshly grated nutmeg

Boil the celeriac with the bay leaves, in a generous amount of salted water for about 30 minutes, until tender. Remove the bay leaves and let the celeriac cool for a bit.

Mash the celeriac or puree it in a food processor until smooth. Add the crème fraîche and thyme leaves. Season the puree with salt, pepper, and nutmeg.

steak & kidney pie

This recipe is for 4 to 6 people, or generous portions for 2 people for a couple of days.

Don't make any faces: The kidneys in this classic recipe are an absolute must and are really good. I make it with stout (preferably Guinness) and lots of vegetables; turnips, celery . . . whatever you have on hand.

If you really don't want to eat kidneys, replace them with more stew meat.

2 tbsp butter
1 onion, diced
7 oz (200 g) veal kidney, cut into
    ¾-inch (2-cm) cubes
1¾ lb (800 g) beef stew meat, cut
    into ¾-inch (2-cm) cubes
¼ cup all-purpose flour
salt and freshly ground black pepper
1 small or ½ big celeriac, cut into
    ¾-inch (2-cm) cubes
3 or 4 turnips or rutabagas, cubed
2 tbsp chopped fresh thyme
3 bay leaves
1 can (15 oz / 33 cl) Guinness (or
    other dark beer or stout)
1½ cups (350 ml) beef broth
3 tbsp Worcestershire sauce
10½ oz (300 g) wild mushrooms,
    cleaned
4 sprigs fresh flat-leaf parsley,
    chopped
6 sheets puff pastry
1 egg, beaten

Preheat the oven to 350°F (180°C).

Melt the butter in a large skillet. Saute the onion until soft but not browned. Dredge the kidney and stew meat pieces in the flour, season with salt and pepper, and add to the pan.

Brown the meat, stirring. Add the vegetables, thyme, and bay leaves. Add the beer, broth, and Worcestershire sauce. Gently bring to a boil. Cover the skillet with the lid askew and place it in the oven.

Bake for 1½ hours, then check the liquid level. You may have to add some broth. You can also add the mushrooms now. Cover and bake for 1 hour longer.

Add the parsley and let the filling cool.

Dust the counter with flour. Roll out the puff pastry into a large slab.

Fill a shallow, 4½-cup (1-l) baking dish or 4 to 6 smaller dishes with the stew and brush the edges of the dish with the beaten egg. Place the dough on top and press the edges firmly. Let the dough hang about 1 inch (2.5 cm) over the edge and trim off the excess dough with a knife.

With a sharp knife, cut a small hole in the center of the crust to allow steam to escape from the pie, so that the dough will be nice and fluffy and won't become soggy.

Scrape the rest of the dough together and roll out again. Cut out leaves (or some other shape that you like), and stick them with some beaten egg along the edges of the dough or around the hole in the middle. Brush all with the beaten egg.

Preheat the oven to 350°F (180°C).

Bake the pie for about 30 minutes, or until golden brown and the filling is boiling.

Serve with mashed potatoes and green vegetables, like haricots verts or green peas.

vol–au–vent filled with creamy celeriac & wild mushrooms with a red onion compote

This is a nice dish if you want a day without meat. The recipe makes about 6 vol-au-vents.

FOR THE COMPOTE

1 large red onion, cut into thin rings

1 tbsp olive oil

2 sprigs fresh rosemary

3 tbsp (50 ml) red wine

2 tbsp raspberry vinegar

1 tbsp ginger syrup from a jar of
preserved ginger

salt and freshly ground black pepper

FOR THE FILLING

4½ cups (1 l) vegetable broth

½ celeriac, peeled and cut into
¾-inch (2-cm) chunks

14 oz (400 g) wild mushrooms,
cleaned and torn or cut into
equal pieces

3 tbsp (50 g) butter

salt and freshly ground black pepper

1 onion, diced

2 large cloves garlic, minced

1 tbsp chopped fresh rosemary

3 tbsp all-purpose flour

⅓ cup (75 ml) crème fraîche

⅓ cup (75 ml) dry sherry or marsala
wine

FOR THE DOUGH

2½ cups (300 g) all-purpose flour

salt

½ cup plus 2 tbsp (150 g) butter

ice water

1 egg, beaten

Make the compote first so that it can cool while you make the rest: Saute the onion in the oil over very low heat, and add the rosemary. When the onion is soft, add the wine, vinegar, and ginger syrup and season with salt and pepper. Simmer over low heat for another 15 minutes, until the ingredients are integrated. Set aside until ready to use.

Make the filling: Bring the broth to a boil. Add the celeriac and simmer until tender. Drain, reserving the broth. Set aside.

Quickly saute the mushrooms in half the butter over high heat. Season with salt and pepper.

Melt the remaining butter in a large pan over medium heat. Add the onion and saute until it begins to brown. Add the garlic and rosemary and saute for 2 minutes. Stir in the flour.

Stir in the broth, cooking and stirring until the sauce is just thicker than yogurt.

Stir in the crème fraîche and sherry. Cook the sauce until it's thick. Stir in the celeriac and mushrooms.

Preheat the oven to 350°F (180°C).

Make the dough: Combine the flour and salt in a bowl and cut in the butter until the mixture resembles a coarse meal. Add a few drops of ice water to make a nice, smooth dough. Wrap it in plastic wrap and let it rest in the fridge for 30 minutes.

Grease 6 small pie plates or 1 large pie plate. Roll out the dough on a well-floured surface to ¼ inch (6 mm) thick. Line the pans with the dough and trim off the excess dough around the edges.

Cut out some decorations from the remaining dough. I like to make stars. Keep the decorations under plastic wrap until ready to use.

Fill the dough with the mushroom filling. Place the stars on the vol-au-vents and brush all with beaten egg.

Bake the vol-au-vents about 25 minutes, until they're golden brown.

Serve with the compote and a green salad.

dublin lawyer

Because lawyers from Dublin are fat, rich, and always drunk . . .

FOR 2 PEOPLE

1 whole, very fresh lobster
3 tbsp butter
¼ cup whiskey
½ cup (125 ml) heavy cream
1 tbsp brown sugar
1 tbsp chopped fresh parsley
salt and freshly ground black pepper

Halve the lobster lengthwise. Remove all the meat from the tail and use a hammer to remove the meat from the claws.

Keep the lobster shell halves and clean them well, as you'll serve the meal in it.

Cube the lobster meat. Heat the butter in a saute pan until it foams, add the lobster meat, and saute quickly until just firm, but not completely white.

Gently heat the whiskey in a saucepan over low heat, then pour it over the lobster meat in the saute pan and carefully ignite the alcohol. Add the cream, stir to make a smooth sauce, and season with the brown sugar, parsley, salt, and pepper.

Spoon the filling into the lobster halves and serve with fluffy white rice or baked potatoes and spinach.

porchetta

This is a ridiculously delicious Italian meal, especially if you love pork belly. It's very easy to make because once it's in the oven there's very little that can go wrong. Italians eat it on the street with some bread, which you can do too. On the next two pages I'll suggest a few side dishes. The side dishes on pages 144–147, which go with the pulled pork, also go really well with this. With this amount of meat you'll have more than enough for 10 to 12 people, and you can prepare an even bigger piece of meat for a party, as you'll certainly make friends with this!

6½ lb (3 kg) pork belly, with the rib still attached because of its meat, and the rind (that is, the skin, which will become nice and crusty—the Brits call it "crackling")

3 tbsp (50 g) coarse sea salt

freshly ground black pepper

1 small bunch fresh thyme, coarsely chopped

1 small bunch fresh rosemary, coarsely chopped

1 bigger bunch fresh sage, coarsely chopped

2 tbsp fennel seed

8 cloves garlic, diced

1 cup (100 g) pine nuts

¼ cup (60 ml) olive oil

Preheat the oven to 450°F (230°C).

Place the pork belly on a large cutting board, skin up. With a small, sharp kitchen knife or craft knife, score the rind from top to bottom, at ⅓-inch (8-mm) intervals. Turn the pork belly over. Sprinkle the salt and pepper over the meat and use your hands to rub it in.

In a food processor or blender, coarsely chop the herbs with the fennel seeds, garlic, and pine nuts. Sprinkle the meat with this mixture.

Cut about 10 pieces of kitchen twine, each 1 foot (30 cm) long, and have them ready nearby.

Roll up the meat and tie it together firmly. Start in the middle and then tie up each end. Then use the rest of the strings in between. Cut off the ends.

Rub half the oil on the meat and rub the entire thing with some more salt and pepper.

Pour the remaining oil in the roasting pan, add the meat, and roast it for 20 minutes.

Lower the oven temperature to 300°F (150°C) and cover the meat with aluminum foil.

Bake for 3 hours, without even looking at it.

Remove the foil and baste the meat with juices from the roasting pan. Roast another 20 minutes, uncovered, to get a nice crackling crust. Remove the meat from the oven and lift it onto a cutting board.

It may stick, so perhaps you'll need to carefully hack it away from the bottom of the pan. Cut the porchetta into thin slices.

Eat warm or cold.

broiled carrots

2¼ lb (1 kg) carrots
1 cup (250 ml) chicken or vegetable
    broth
3 tbsp (50 g) seeded butter
    (page 20)
9 oz (250 g) shallots, sliced
1 tbsp fresh thyme leaves
½ tsp freshly grated nutmeg
1 tbsp brown sugar

Peel the carrots and halve them lengthwise.

Heat the broth and boil the carrots in it for 15 minutes, until tender. Drain.

Preheat the broiler.

Melt the seeded butter in a wide broiler-proof pan. Saute the shallots until they are translucent, then add the carrots. Sprinkle with the thyme and nutmeg.

Stir in the brown sugar and briefly caramelize under the hot broiler. Serve immediately.

parsnip & apple compote

1 lb (500 g) parsnips, peeled
1 lb (500 g) apples, peeled, cored,
    and cubed
1 tbsp butter
salt and freshly ground black pepper
pinch of cinnamon
pinch of freshly grated nutmeg
1 tbsp brown sugar (optional)

In a large saucepan of boiling water, boil the parsnips until tender. In a separate saucepan, boil the apples in a small amount of water until tender. Drain the parsnips and add to the apples. Mash them into a coarse puree and stir in the butter, salt and pepper, spices, and brown sugar, if desired.

Serve with the porchetta on page 181 or with duck.

Camargue

toad in a hole with red onion

Toad in a hole is a traditional British recipe made with small sausages, but here I replace them with roasted onion. You can also make this with baked sausages: Roll them up in bacon slices—oohh, that's really good. (By the way, for this picture I baked these toads in individual ramekins, which makes them look quite pretty.)

4 medium-sized red onions, peeled
⅓ cup plus 2 tbsp (100 ml) olive oil

FOR THE BATTER
1¼ cups (300 ml) milk
1 cup (125 g) all-purpose flour
3 eggs
fresh thyme and/or rosemary
pinch of salt and freshly ground
    black pepper

Preheat the oven to 475°F (250°C).

Place the onions next to one another in a baking dish and pour the olive oil on top. Place the baking dish just below the center of the oven and bake for 15 minutes.

Make the batter: Whisk all the ingredients in a large glass measuring cup or pitcher until smooth. Open the oven door and pour the batter into the dish. Be careful, as it can splatter! The batter will immediately solidify in the hot oil, quite exciting.

Bake the toad in a hole for 20 minutes without opening the oven.

Once you've taken it out of the oven, let it cool for a bit; it will settle.

Serve plain, with some chutney from page 130, or with a salad.

fresh salad with endive, apple, pomegranate & buttermilk dressing

FOR THE DRESSING
½ cup (125 g) mayonnaise
3 tbsp crème fraîche
⅓ cup (80 ml) buttermilk
1 tbsp diced shallot
1 tbsp cider vinegar
1 clove garlic, minced
pinch of salt
freshly ground black pepper

FOR THE SALAD
3 or 4 heads Belgian endive, ends
   and outer leaves removed
1 red apple
juice of 1 lemon
1 handful flat-leaf parsley
seeds from ½ pomegranate (about
   ¼ cup / 50 g)

Whisk together all the dressing ingredients. Put the dressing in the fridge until use.

Pull all the leaves from the endives. Cube the apple. Toss the endive and apple in a bowl and sprinkle with lemon juice. Stir in the parsley and sprinkle the salad with pomegranate seeds.

Drizzle the dressing over the salad.

oxtail stew & beluga lentils

Oxtail has never been in the spotlight. That's too bad, as it's inexpensive and has a very rich flavor. You'll need to pull the meat from the bones after cooking, but that, I hope, won't keep you from making this recipe.

FOR THE STEW
3 lb (1.5 kg) oxtail, in big chunks (ask your butcher to cut it)
3 tbsp all-purpose flour
salt and freshly ground black pepper
3 or 4 tbsp olive oil
2 onions, diced
2 garlic cloves, minced
2 carrots, cubed
2 stalks celery, cubed
2 (28-oz / 800-g) cans whole peeled tomatoes
5 sprigs fresh thyme, or 1 tsp dried thyme
2 bay leaves
1¼ cups (300 ml) red wine
about 2¼ cups (500 ml) beef broth
1⅓ cups (200 g) beluga or Puy lentils
1 tbsp chopped fresh parsley (optional)

FOR THE POLENTA
2 cups (300 g) polenta
salt
½ cup plus 2 tbsp (150 g) butter
freshly ground black pepper

Preheat the oven to 300°F (150°C).

Rinse the oxtail and pat it dry with paper towels. Trim away as much fat as possible. Put the oxtail in a bowl and sprinkle with flour, salt, and pepper. Toss briefly so that all chunks are coated.

Heat 2 tbsp of the oil in a large ovenproof skillet. Brown the oxtail over medium heat. You may have to do it in 2 or 3 batches, depending on the size of your pan.

Add the onions, garlic, carrots, and celery. Saute for about 10 minutes on low heat and add the tomatoes, thyme, and bay leaves.

Return any extra oxtail pieces to the pan and add the wine and enough broth to cover the oxtail. Season with salt and pepper.

Bring to a boil, cover, and place the pan in the oven. Bake for 3 hours, stirring after 1½ hours. After 2½ hours, add the lentils and stir well. After 3 hours, the meat should fall off the bones and the sauce should be thick.

Scoop the meat out of the sauce and let cool. With a big spoon, skim as much fat as possible off the surface of the sauce. Pull the meat off the bones and add it to the sauce.

Make the polenta: Bring 4½ cups (1 l) generously salted water to a boil in a large saucepan.

When the water boils, add the polenta in a thin trickle, stirring constantly with a whisk.

Keep stirring until the polenta thickens. Lower the heat and let the polenta simmer for about 30 minutes, stirring occasionally. Be careful, as polenta can splatter.

Stir in the butter, season with pepper, and divide the polenta among 4 plates.

Ladle the oxtail stew on top. Sprinkle with chopped parsley, if desired. You could also replace the polenta with mashed potatoes. Or even buttered tagliatelle.

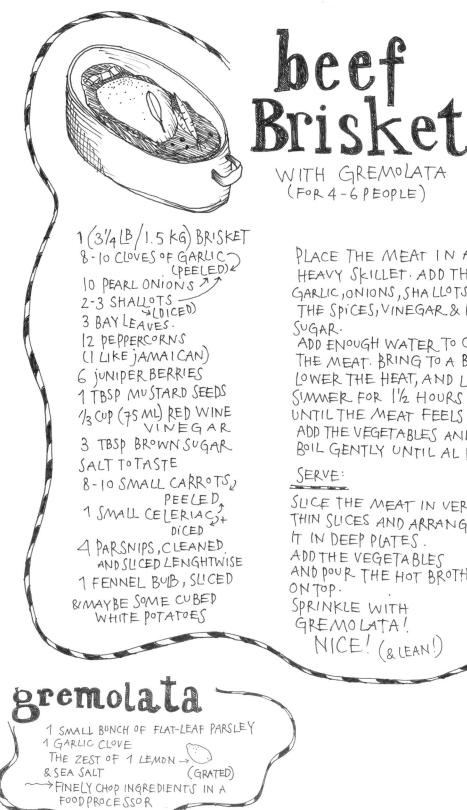

beef Brisket

WITH GREMOLATA
(FOR 4 - 6 PEOPLE)

1 (3¼ LB / 1.5 KG) BRISKET
8 - 10 CLOVES OF GARLIC
(PEELED)
10 PEARL ONIONS
2 - 3 SHALLOTS (DICED)
3 BAY LEAVES.
12 PEPPERCORNS
(I LIKE JAMAICAN)
6 JUNIPER BERRIES
1 TBSP MUSTARD SEEDS
⅓ CUP (75 ML) RED WINE VINEGAR
3 TBSP BROWN SUGAR
SALT TO TASTE
8 - 10 SMALL CARROTS, PEELED
1 SMALL CELERIAC, DICED
4 PARSNIPS, CLEANED. AND SLICED LENGHTWISE
1 FENNEL BULB, SLICED
& MAYBE SOME CUBED WHITE POTATOES

PLACE THE MEAT IN A HEAVY SKILLET. ADD THE GARLIC, ONIONS, SHALLOTS, ALL THE SPICES, VINEGAR & BROWN SUGAR.
ADD ENOUGH WATER TO COVER THE MEAT. BRING TO A BOIL, LOWER THE HEAT, AND LET SIMMER FOR 1½ HOURS OR UNTIL THE MEAT FEELS FIRM. ADD THE VEGETABLES AND BOIL GENTLY UNTIL AL DENTE.

SERVE:

SLICE THE MEAT IN VERY THIN SLICES AND ARRANGE IT IN DEEP PLATES.
ADD THE VEGETABLES AND POUR THE HOT BROTH ON TOP.
SPRINKLE WITH GREMOLATA!
NICE! (& LEAN!)

gremolata

1 SMALL BUNCH OF FLAT-LEAF PARSLEY
1 GARLIC CLOVE
THE ZEST OF 1 LEMON
& SEA SALT   (GRATED)
FINELY CHOP INGREDIENTS IN A FOOD PROCESSOR

ST.PATRICK'S DAY

17 MARCH IS ST. PATRICK'S DAY IN IRELAND.
A VERY FESTIVE DAY, COMPARABLE TO QUEEN'S DAY IN
THE NETHERLANDS. WE WOULD WEAR GREEN CLOTHES
TO SCHOOL AND PRACTICE FOLK DANCES IN CLASS: HEELS,
TOE, HEELS, TOE . . . ON THE DAY OF THE BIG PARADE
THROUGH DOWNTOWN DUBLIN I WOULD GET A PIN WITH
THE IRISH FLAG AND A MEDALLION WITH ST. PATRICK,
AND I'D IMMEDIATELY PIN IT TO MY GREEN COAT. SITTING
ON THE SHOULDERS OF MY UNCLE JAAP, WHO MADE RADIO
DOCUMENTARIES, I WOULD REPORT ON THE PARADE FOR
DUTCH RADIO. AND IN THE EVENING WE WOULD EAT IRISH STEW. THE
ADULTS WOULD DRINK GUINNESS AND WE KIDS NEON-GREEN LEMONADE.

irish stew

1 tsp butter
14 oz (400 g) boneless lamb
    stew meat, in chunks (I use leg
    of lamb)
1 large onion, diced
3 ribs celery, chopped
2 leeks, white and light green parts,
    washed well and sliced into
    rounds
1 parsnip, peeled and cubed
2 carrots, peeled and cubed
½ rutabaga, peeled and cubed
salt and freshly ground black pepper
about 9 cups (2 l) lamb broth
    (or chicken broth)
a few sprigs of fresh thyme
2 bay leaves
2 potatoes, peeled and cubed
    (optional)
½ cup (100 g) barley
1 small bunch fresh parsley, chopped

Melt the butter in a large saute pan over medium-high heat. Add
the lamb and brown it on all sides. Add the onion, celery, leeks,
parsnip, carrots, and rutabaga and saute for about 15 minutes.
Season generously with salt and pepper.

Add enough broth to cover everything generously, then add the
thyme and bay leaves.

Bring to a boil, then lower the heat and simmer for 1½ to 2 hours,
until the lamb is very tender. The cooking time depends on the
quality of the meat.

When it's almost done, about half hour before serving, add the
potatoes, if using, and the barley. Cook until tender.

Sprinkle the stew generously with parsley and serve with a nice
piece of soda bread (page 23).

It tastes even better the next day.

turbot tower with nutty white cabbage and vanilla beurre blanc

It's quite a meal, this. Turbot is expensive and not always easy to get. Feel free to replace it with sea bass, or even a piece of cod. And oh, leave the skin on: It keeps the tender fish from falling apart.

FOR THE CABBAGE
½ cup plus 2 tbsp (150 g) butter
⅔ head green cabbage, thinly sliced
2 bay leaves
about 1¼ cups (300 ml) white wine
salt and freshly ground black pepper

FOR THE TURBOT
a few tbsp all-purpose flour
salt and freshly ground black pepper
6 (5-oz / 150-g) pieces turbot fillet
1 tbsp butter
1 tbsp oil
a few sprigs of fresh flat-leaf parsley

FOR THE BEURRE BLANC
2 shallots, diced
1 bay leaf
¾ cup (200 ml) white wine
½ cup (125 g) crème fraîche
1 cup (225 g) cold butter, cut into
    cubes
seeds from 1 vanilla bean

Make the cabbage: Melt the butter in a large saucepan over medium heat. Let the butter brown, but not burn. When it gives off a nutmeglike aroma and is the color of tea, add the cabbage. Keep stirring and lower the heat. Add the bay leaves and wine. Cover and braise the cabbage until tender, at least 35 minutes. Stir occasionally. Add a little water if the mixture becomes too dry. Season with salt and pepper and set aside.

Make the turbot: Combine the flour with the salt and pepper in a shallow bowl and dredge the fish in the flour. Shake off any extra flour.

Heat the butter and oil in a nonstick saute pan. Once it's hot, put the fillets in the pan, skin side down, and don't touch them until the edges are nicely browned and crisp, about 6 minutes. Only then may you turn the fish. The turbot needs to be cooked for only 2 minutes on the other side.

Make the beurre blanc: Heat the shallots, bay leaf, and wine in a small saucepan. Over low heat, cook until the liquid is reduced to about ¼ cup. Strain into a bowl (discard the solids) and pour the liquid back into the pan. Place the saucepan over medium heat and add the crème fraîche. Then whisk in the butter a little at a time, keeping the sauce close to a boil but never boiling, and whisk in the vanilla seeds.

Once all the butter is incorporated, the sauce should be nice and thick.

Ladle a spoonful of sauce on a (preheated) plate, add a spoonful of cabbage on top, and place a piece of fried fish on top. Garnish with parsley.

Serve immediately with a fresh and simple green salad or some steamed spinach.

daube provençale

When we're in Provence for the summer, I get bombarded with the most varied, often traditional, family recipes. Most of the time, because winter is so short there, these recipes are for summer meals (you'll see them soon). But I can give you this winter recipe now. It's delicious.

Since you marinate the meat for 24 hours in an acidic marinade (orange juice and red wine), you can really use any kind of meat: The lesser-quality cuts are perfectly fine choices. I make it with beef, but you can also use lamb or mutton. It will all be tender and tasty.

3 lb (1.5 kg) beef: chuck, brisket, shank, whatever there is, in pieces

1 (750-ml) bottle Côte du Rhône, or a Vacqueyras, Gigondas, or red Minervois (It really does matter which wine you choose. Especially for this meal!)

salt and freshly ground black pepper

3 sprigs fresh thyme

2 bay leaves

3 carrots, peeled and sliced

1 orange, washed well and cut into 8 wedges

1 large onion, cut into rings

2 cloves garlic, sliced

olive oil

1 small (6-oz / 170-g) can tomato paste

3½ oz (100 g) pitted black olives

Place the meat in a big bowl. Add the wine, salt and pepper, thyme, bay leaves, carrots, orange, onion, and garlic. Let marinate for ideally 24 hours, but at least 12.

Scoop the meat out of the marinade and remove any onions that have stuck to the meat. Put the onions back in the marinade. Heat a splash of olive oil in a heavy cast-iron skillet and fry the meat in batches until it is browned all over. Set the meat aside.

Pour the marinade into a large saucepan or stew pot and bring it to a boil. Boil it down for 5 minutes and skim any foam from the surface. Put the meat back in the pan, add 4½ cups (1 l) water, and stir in the tomato paste.

Cover the pan and let it stew on low heat for about 3 hours. Stop by at times to stir it.

Add the olives 15 minutes before the stew is ready. Taste for salt and pepper.

If the sauce is too thin, you can reduce it by boiling the stew on high heat without a lid.

Serve with mashed potatoes, rice, or pasta. I like the stew with the sweet potato mash with green cabbage & parsnips on page 164. This isn't officially French, but *soit.*

The neighbors across the street in Amsterdam

The neighbors across the street in Paris

Wicklow Mountains

DESSERT

sticky chocolate cake in your coffee mug in 3 minutes

Yes, for real! This is ready in three minutes. I don't like to cook in the microwave, but in this case it's very appealing. Especially when you're home alone and you suddenly have an irresistible craving for chocolate but don't feel like doing much work.

I can imagine, however, that some of you might have trouble with the idea of making a cake in a microwave. If you prefer to use a conventional oven, use self-rising flour instead of all-purpose flour and bake at 350°F (180°C) in a greased ovenproof cup for about 20 minutes.

3 tbsp all-purpose flour
3 tbsp sugar
1½ tbsp unsweetened cocoa powder
1 sachet (2 tsp) vanilla sugar
1 egg
3 tbsp milk
3 tbsp sunflower oil

IF YOU WISH
3 tbsp chocolate chips or grated
    chocolate
3 tbsp raisins

Mix the dry ingredients in the coffee mug. Add the egg and whisk with a fork. Add the milk and oil and whisk some more.

Then stir in the chocolate chips or raisins, if desired. Place the mug in the microwave and "bake" the batter for 3 minutes on high.

The cake will rise above the rim of the mug, but that's fine! Let it cool for a bit.

If you wish, add any syrup, such as *appelstroop* or golden syrup, a dash of liqueur, or serve with vanilla ice cream.

205

upside-down pear & nut tart with calvados syrup

Before I lived in Amsterdam, I lived in The Hague while attending art school. To make some extra money I worked in restaurants, in the kitchen or as a waitress. In one of the restaurants (Peppermint; you may have heard of it), we'd bake this tart weekly. A hundred years later I still find this a great recipe, and I'm giving it to you—I noted it down in my very, very first recipe journal, which I made with my colleagues Natascha and Iris.

We used to eat it with maple syrup, but I make a more grown-up version now, with Calvados syrup. Try it: You won't regret it.

FOR THE TART
¼ cup (50 g) granulated sugar
4 firm-ripe pears (any kind will do because you'll cook them down completely)
1 cup (225 g) packed light brown sugar
1 cup plus 2 tbsp (250 g) butter, plus more for the pan
4 eggs
2 cups (250 g) self-rising flour
⅓ cup plus 2 tbsp (100 ml) milk
1¼ cups (150 g) chopped walnuts, plus about 8 walnut halves for garnish

FOR THE CALVADOS SYRUP
2 cups (400 g) sugar
3 tbsp (50 g) butter
3 tbsp Calvados

Make the tart: Preheat the oven to 325°F (160°C). Butter a deep, 9-inch (22-cm) round cake pan, line the bottom with a round of parchment paper, and butter the parchment paper thickly with butter. Sprinkle the granulated sugar over the butter.

Peel, quarter, and core the pears. Arrange them in the bottom of the pan with the cut sides up.

In a large bowl, beat the brown sugar and butter until creamy, then beat in the eggs one at a time. Sift in the flour and beat until combined, then stir in the milk and chopped nuts.

Pour the batter over the pears in the pan and bake about 1 hour, until a bamboo skewer inserted in the center comes out clean and dry.

Let the tart cool completely in the pan, then gently invert it onto a plate and carefully peel off the parchment paper.

Garnish the top of the tart with the reserved walnuts.

Make the Calvados syrup: Heat the sugar in a heavy saucepan over low heat. The sugar will melt slowly. Shake the pan gently; the edges will color first. Be careful of splatter; melted sugar is super hot!

Remove from the heat and add ½ cup (150 ml) water; the sugar will splatter—watch out!

Return the pan to the heat and stir gently until it forms a smooth sauce. Stir in the butter. Take the sauce off the heat, let it cool for a bit, and stir in the Calvados. Pour a little sauce over the tart, so that it can be absorbed.

Serve the rest of the sauce in a little jug. You can keep the sauce for a day or three in the fridge, just heat it up before you serve.

lace crêpes with cardamom ice cream

FOR ABOUT 10 PEOPLE

FOR THE CARDAMOM ICE CREAM
1¼ cups (300 ml) milk
1 vanilla bean, split and scraped of
seeds
2 egg yolks
⅓ cup (75 g) superfine sugar
2 tbsp freshly ground cardamom
seeds
1¼ cups (300 ml) heavy cream

FOR THE CRÊPES
1⅔ cups (200 g) all-purpose flour
pinch of salt
2 sachets (4 tsp) vanilla sugar
2 eggs
3 cups (750 ml) milk
butter for the pan

FOR GARNISH
confectioners' sugar
ground cardamom (optional)

Make the cardamom ice cream: In a medium saucepan, bring the milk almost to a boil. Add the vanilla bean and the seeds and set aside to steep for 10 minutes.

In a medium bowl, whisk the egg yolks with the superfine sugar until foamy white. Strain the milk mixture into the egg yolk mixture and stir thoroughly.

Pour the mixture back into the saucepan and stir on low heat until it thickens to the consistency of yogurt. Stir in the cardamom. Let the mixture (a crème anglaise) cool completely.

In a medium bowl, whip the cream until firm peaks form, then fold it into the cooled crème anglaise. Pour into an airtight container and place in the freezer for at least 4 hours.

Make the crêpes: Combine the flour, salt, and vanilla sugar in a large bowl and make a well in the center. Break the eggs into the well and add half of the milk. Whisk into a smooth batter. While stirring, add the rest of the milk.

Melt about 1 tsp butter in a nonstick skillet over medium heat until light brown. With a big spoon, ladle thin stripes of batter in a checkered pattern into the pan. Cook the crêpe until it is golden brown, then turn it and brown the other side. Repeat. Layer the crêpes on a plate, separated with plastic wrap or aluminum foil and cover them with a lid so they remain nice and soft. Continue until all the batter is used and all the crêpes are cooked.

Serve a crêpe on each plate. With an ice-cream spoon, scoop a generous serving of cardamom ice cream onto each crêpe. Sprinkle lavishly with confectioners' sugar and, if you wish, with some extra ground cardamom. Attack immediately.

white chocolate coffee

When I studied in Antwerp, a girlfriend and I would frequent the café Witzli Putzli around the corner for hot chocolate—real chocolate, with whipped cream, ground cardamom, and a generous drizzle of golden syrup. I would save money for it so that I could go as often as possible, even, sometimes, alone. It was so ridiculously good.

This is my own variation on that hot chocolate. You can serve it with golden syrup, but it might be too sweet with this version.

2 cups (500 ml) whole milk
3½ oz (100 g) chopped white
    chocolate
1⅔ cups (400 ml) strong hot coffee
½ cup plus 2 tbsp (150 ml) heavy
    cream
1 sachet (2 tsp) vanilla sugar
1 tsp freshly ground cardamom seeds

In a small saucepan, heat the milk almost to a boil. Take the milk off the heat and stir in the white chocolate. Wait 5 minutes and stir again; the chocolate will have melted now. Stir in the hot coffee. In a medium bowl, whip the cream with the vanilla sugar until thick.

Pour the chocolate coffee into 4 mugs and spoon the whipped cream on top. Sprinkle with cardamom and serve immediately.

Wicklow Mountains

X*MAS

CHRISTMAS IS DECEMBER 25,
BUT IT WAS IN SEPTEMBER THAT THE HOUSEWIVES ON OUR
STREET BEGAN TO MAKE THE PLUM PUDDING. THEY HAD
TO START FAR IN ADVANCE BECAUSE THEY WOULD
NEED TO POUR LIQUOR OVER THE PUDDING EVERY
WEEK FOR THREE MONTHS TO LET IT SEEP IN.
ON CHRISTMAS, THEY WOULD COOK THE
PLUM PUDDING AGAIN AND THEN THEY WOULD
IGNITE IT. DESPITE THE FACT THAT WE CHILDREN
WEREN'T ALLOWED TO EAT THE PLUM PUDDING
(DUE TO THE ENORMOUS AMOUNT OF ALCOHOL IT
CONTAINED), WE THOUGHT IT WAS THE COOLEST
THING EVER: A BURNING DESSERT IN THE DARK.

(quick) plum pudding

¾ cup (100 g) all-purpose flour
1 tsp *speculaaskruiden* (see Note)
1 tsp cinnamon
1 tsp ground ginger
pinch of freshly grated nutmeg
pinch of salt
1⅓ cups (100 g) fresh white bread
    crumbs or 1 cup (100 g) plain
    dried bread crumbs
½ cup (100 g) packed dark brown
    sugar
½ cup plus 2 tbsp (150 g) cold butter
1 cup (150 g) raisins
1 cup (150 g) currants
⅓ cup (50 g) chopped mixed
    candied fruit
⅔ cup (100 g) chopped dates
2 tbsp (50 g) honey or golden syrup
grated zest and juice of 1 lemon
2 eggs, beaten
¼ cup (60 ml) brandy

Preheat the oven to 350°F (180°C). Place a big roasting pan filled three-quarters full of water on the rack just below the center. Butter two 2-cup (500-ml) pudding molds.

Sift the flour with the spices and the salt into a large bowl, then stir in the bread crumbs and brown sugar. Rub in the butter until the mixture resembles a coarse meal.

Stir in the raisins, currants, candied fruit, and dates.

Whisk the rest of the ingredients together in a separate bowl and add them to the flour mixture. Fill the prepared molds with the batter to ⅜ inch (1 cm) below the top.

Cover each mold with a round of parchment paper cut to size and wrap the entire pudding with a double layer of aluminum foil.

Put the puddings in the water-filled roasting pan in the oven and bake them for 2½ hours.

Open the aluminum foil, prick holes in the pudding with a bamboo skewer, and, if you want to preserve it, pour some liquor over it every few days—brandy, whiskey, whatever you have. Leave the pudding in the molds, covered well with foil. It will keep for several weeks. To reheat the pudding, wrap it completely in foil and heat for 20 minutes at 350°F (180°C).

But! You can also serve the pudding immediately. Remove the foil and parchment paper and invert the pudding onto a nice plate. Pour brandy caramel sauce over it or serve with unsweetened whipped cream.

Note: *Speculaaskruiden* is a combination of ground spices, usually equal parts cinnamon, coriander, nutmeg, cloves, ginger, and cardamom, plus some dried grated orange peel. For a quick substitute, I suggest: ¼ tsp coriander, ¼ tsp ground cloves, and ¼ tsp cardamom.

brandy caramel sauce

7 tbsp (100 g) unsalted butter
grated zest of 1 orange
½ cup (100 g) sugar
3 tbsp brandy

Melt the butter with the orange zest and the sugar in a saucepan. Cook over low heat, gently swirling the pan occasionally until the caramel turns the color of tea. Be gentle, don't stir too much, and it will be fine.

Pour in the brandy, remove from the heat, and stir until it's a smooth sauce. WATCH OUT! It can splatter for a bit, and caramel is very hot!

île flottante with mocha crème anglaise and nutmeg

FOR THE CARAMEL
1 cup (200 g) sugar
1 tbsp butter

FOR THE CRÈME ANGLAISE
⅓ cup (75 g) sugar
5 egg yolks
2 cups (500 ml) milk
1 vanilla bean, split and scraped of
    seeds
1 shot of strong brewed espresso or
    1 sachet (2 tsp) instant espresso
    granules

FOR THE "ISLANDS"
5 egg whites
pinch of salt
½ cup plus 2 tbsp (125 g) superfine
    sugar

AND FURTHER
½ cup (50 g) sliced almonds
freshly grated nutmeg

Make the caramel: Heat the sugar in a heavy saucepan and add 3 tbsp water. Don't stir. Let the sugar melt and stir in the butter (with a wooden spoon!) only once the sugar begins to color at the edges. Take the caramel off the heat when it has turned the color of tea.

Be careful with this next step especially, as the caramel is really very hot.

Place a sheet of parchment paper on the counter and pour the caramel from a great height in a thin drizzle up and down, up and down in a checkered pattern. Let it cool.

Make the crème anglaise: In a large bowl, whisk the sugar with the egg yolks until foamy.

In a medium saucepan over very low heat, heat the milk, the vanilla pod and seeds, and the espresso for about 20 minutes. Strain the mixture into a bowl, then drizzle it into the egg mixture, stirring constantly. Pour the mixture back into the saucepan and heat the sauce gently, stirring. Don't let it become too hot, or the egg will curdle.

The sauce is ready when it's thick enough to coat the back of a wooden spoon. Let it cool and then refrigerate until use.

Make the "islands": Whisk the egg whites in a clean bowl until stiff peaks form. Add a pinch of salt and, while beating, add the superfine sugar bit by bit until all the sugar is dissolved.

Heat a large saucepan of water almost to a boil. With two serving spoons, form big "clouds" of egg white mixture. Gently set them in the water and poach for 2 minutes. Flip them with a skimmer and poach another 2 minutes. Take the "islands" out of the water and let them drain on a clean towel.

Briefly toast the almonds in a dry skillet until they are golden brown.

Pour the crème anglaise into a nice big bowl or into deep plates and set the islands in the middle.

Break the caramel grid and place a piece on every island.

Sprinkle the *îles flottantes* with the almonds and nutmeg.

217

pears with goat's milk brie & red wine jelly

Of course, instead of goat's milk brie you may use regular brie, or goat cheese. Even blue cheese! Any of those would be good here.

1 (750-ml) bottle of red wine
1¼ cups (250 g) sugar
4 cloves
3 star anise
6 to 8 cardamom pods
2 cinnamon sticks
4 Comice pears, peeled and halved, with the stems left on
6 sheets gelatin, or 2 tbsp unflavored powdered gelatin
10 oz (300 g) goat's milk brie
¼ cup (85 g) honey

In a large saucepan over very low heat, combine the red wine, sugar, cloves, star anise, cardamom, and cinnamon sticks. Add the pears and poach them until they are soft but still hold their shape. Take them out of the syrup with a slotted spoon and let them cool.

Continue to boil the cooking liquid until it's reduced by half.

Reserve 2 cups (500 ml) of the syrup in a pitcher and set the rest aside (it won't be much, just a few spoonfuls).

If using gelatin sheets, soak them in cold water until soft, then remove them from the water and squeeze out the excess water. Strain the 2 cups (500 ml) of wine syrup into a saucepan, heat it over low heat, and add the soaked or powdered gelatin, stirring to dissolve. Let the syrup cool a bit, then pour it into a shallow rectangular pan and let the jelly solidify for 4 hours in the fridge.

Preheat the broiler.

Place the pears cut side up on a baking sheet and place very thinly sliced goat's milk brie on half of them.

Broil the pear halves briefly, until the brie has just melted. Arrange the pears with the cheese on 4 plates and place the other pear halves (without cheese) next to them.

Ladle a spoonful of the leftover sauce over them.

With a cutter, cut shapes out of the jelly and serve them alongside the pears.

banoffee pie

Okay, this is sweet (even though my version of this classic dessert isn't as sweet as most). But it's so good and can be made so quickly, especially if you have the caramel made in advance. I always make a few cans at a time—they keep forever in the fridge.

If you have unexpected visitors, this is the dessert with which you would spoil them. It will make them love you even more and you, in turn, will love this recipe even more.

FOR THE CARAMEL
1 (14-oz / 400-g) can sweetened
    condensed milk

FOR THE CRUST
1¾ cups (225 g) all-purpose flour
pinch of salt
7 tbsp (100 g) butter, plus extra for
    greasing
a few drops of ice water

FOR THE FILLING
3 bananas
½ cup (100 g) mascarpone
¾ cup (200 ml) heavy cream
2 tbsp confectioners' sugar
dark chocolate to grate over the pie
    (optional)

YOU CAN MAKE NICE CURLS WITH A PEELER

Make the caramel: Put the unopened can of condensed milk in a saucepan filled with plenty of water, cover, and boil for 3 hours. Add more water as necessary to make sure the can remains under water constantly. It can explode otherwise—really!

Let the can cool completely. The milk in the can has now changed into a thick caramel.

Make the crust: Combine the flour, salt, and butter in a food processor and process into a coarse meal (or cut the butter in swiftly with cold hands). Trickle in ice water until the dough just sticks together. Don't knead too long.

Wrap the dough in plastic wrap and let it rest for about 30 minutes in the fridge.

Preheat the oven to 350°F (180°C). Butter a 9½-inch (24-cm) pie pan.

Roll out the dough on a floured surface and line the pan with the dough. Trim off any excess. With a fork, prick holes all over the bottom of the crust.

Bake until golden brown, about 30 minutes.

Let the crust cool completely. You can do all this a day in advance.

Fill the pie: Spread the entire can of caramel in the pie crust. Peel the bananas, slice them, and arrange them over the caramel.

In a medium bowl, beat the mascarpone with the cream and powdered sugar until stiff.

Cover the pie with a generous layer of the cream filling.

Grate some chocolate over it, if you like, but you don't have to. It's good as it is—trust me.

Wicklow, Ireland

clafoutis, basic recipe

There's really no need to make clafoutis only in summer with cherries. The full, creamy flavor of the custard goes really well with wintry ingredients. It's also a dessert that can be made in a snap, and most of the time with ingredients you already have on hand.

2 handfuls of cherries or other dried
    or fresh fruits of your choice
something alcoholic
    (if using dried fruits)
3 eggs
1 cup (250 ml) milk
5 tbsp (75 g) soft butter, plus more
    for greasing
½ cup plus 2 tbsp (125 g) granulated
    sugar
⅔ cup (75 g) all-purpose flour
seeds from 1 vanilla bean, or 1 sachet
    (2 tsp) vanilla sugar
pinch of salt
confectioners' sugar for garnish

Let the dried fruit soak in the spirit or liqueur for 30 minutes, or dice the fresh fruit.

Preheat the oven to 350°F (180°C).

Butter various small baking dishes (or 1 large one) generously with butter. You can use all kinds of sizes, as long as they have a total volume of about 3 cups

In a food processor or bowl, process or whisk the eggs, milk, butter, sugar, flour, vanilla seeds, and salt into a smooth batter.

Pour the batter into the baking dishes and arrange the fruit on top (without the soaking liquid).

Bake the clafoutis for about 25 minutes, until set.

Let it cool (the clafoutis will sink a little) and sprinkle them with confectioners' sugar.

OH, if you're making the recipe for children and you don't wish to use alcohol, replace it with orange juice or tea.

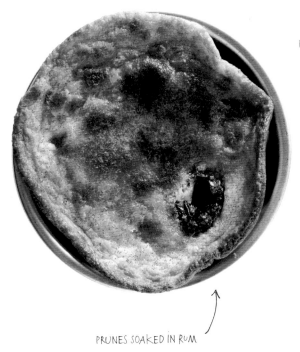

PRUNES SOAKED IN RUM

PEARS, WALNUTS &
BRANDY-SOAKED RAISINS

CLAFOUTIS
WITH CRANBERRIES

BOIL 9 OZ (250 G)
FRESH CRANBERRIES
WITH ½ CUP + 2 TBSP
(125 G) SUGAR &
¾ CUP + 1 TBSP (200 ML)
MARSALA WINE
FOR 7 MIN. UNTIL
MOST OF THE BERRIES
HAVE BURST.

ADD ½ TSP
GROUND
CINNAMON

FILL BUTTERED BAKING DISHES
(OR 1 BIG DISH) WITH
CLAFOUTIS MIXTURE &
ARRANGE CRANBERRIES
ON TOP. (DON'T ADD THE JUICE.)

SPRINKLE THE CLAFOUTIS
WITH CONFECTIONERS'
SUGAR BEFORE SERVING

winter pudding with marsala–raisin custard

Perhaps you know the dish called summer pudding. If not, then sit tight: I'll give you the recipe soon. This is my winter variation.

FOR THE CUSTARD
⅓ cup (50 g) raisins
⅓ cup (75 ml) marsala wine
3 egg yolks
2 tbsp sugar
1 tsp all-purpose flour
1¼ cups (300 ml) milk

FOR THE PUDDING
6 sweet-tart apples (I use Braeburn
   or Elstar, but you can use Fuji)
⅓ cup (60 g) sugar
1 tbsp fresh thyme leaves
3 tbsp (50 g) butter, plus extra for
   greasing
7 slices white bread

Make the custard: Put the raisins in a small bowl, cover them with the marsala, and let them soak for an hour or so.

In a large bowl, beat the egg yolks with the sugar and flour until nice and creamy. In a saucepan, heat the milk almost to a boil. Strain the hot milk into the egg mixture, while stirring. Return everything to the saucepan and slowly bring it to a boil. Let the mixture thicken until it's like yogurt. Take the pan off the heat and add the marsala raisins and the remaining liquid. Stir them in and leave the custard to cool.

Make the pudding: Preheat the oven to 350°F (180°C).

Peel and core the apples and cut them into pieces. In a large saucepan, combine the chunks of apple with the sugar, 3 tbsp water, thyme, and butter and bring all to a boil. Lower the heat and let the apples simmer until they're just about tender but retain their shape, about 20 minutes.

Butter a 2-cup (500-ml) baking dish or pudding mold.

Cut the crusts from 5 slices of the bread. Halve them lengthwise. Arrange them like overlapping shingles on the sides of the mold. With a glass as a guide, cut a circle from another slice and cover the bottom. Fill the mold with the apple mixture. Cut the last slice of bread into a circle and use it to cover the top.

Bake the pudding about 25 minutes, until golden brown. Let it rest for 5 minutes, then invert it onto a pretty plate.

Serve immediately with the cold custard.

salty sticky toffee puddings

What is it with sticky toffee pudding: so deliciously appealing and at the same time much too sweet. Tomorrow will be a healthy day …

FOR THE CARAMEL SAUCE

2 cups (450 g) packed light brown sugar
½ cup plus 1 tbsp (125 g) butter
½ tsp salt
2 cups (500 ml) heavy cream
2 tbsp dark rum or Cognac

FOR THE CAKES

7 oz (200 g) pitted dates, coarsely chopped
1¾ cup (225 g) self-rising flour
pinch of salt
3 tbsp (50 g) butter, at room temperature, plus extra for greasing
1½ cups (300 g) packed light brown sugar
1 egg

Make the caramel sauce: Stir the brown sugar with the butter and the salt in a heavy saucepan over medium heat until the butter is melted. (The mixture will be a little grainy.) Add the cream and bring to a boil.

Simmer, stirring constantly, until the mixture is thick enough to coat the back of a spoon, about 30 minutes.

Take the pan off the heat and let the sauce cool off almost completely. Then stir in the rum or cognac.

Cover the sauce and let it cool in the fridge.

Make the cakes: Bring the dates and 1 cup (250 ml) water to a boil in a small saucepan and cook until the dates are very soft, about 5 minutes. Take them off the heat and let them cool to room temperature, stirring occasionally.

Preheat the oven to 350°F (180°C).

Butter 12 muffin cups.

Sift the flour and salt into a bowl. Beat the butter and sugar in another bowl until creamy and light colored. Beat in the egg. Fold the flour and dates in batches into the butter mixture. Divide the batter among the muffin cups.

Bake the cakes for 25 minutes, or until a bamboo skewer inserted in one comes out dry. Let them rest in the pan on a rack for 10 minutes. Cover a baking sheet with parchment paper and invert the cakes onto it. Place them slightly apart and pour 2 tbsp caramel sauce over each cake.

Let cool completely. (You can do this easily a day in advance and store them in an airtight container until you need them.)

Before serving, preheat the oven to 350°F (180°C).

Bake the soaked cakes for 10 minutes and serve them with cold caramel sauce and unsweetened cream, crème fraîche or vanilla ice cream.

So damn good.

apple blackberry crumble with muesli topping

3 or 4 large apples (I use Honeycrisp, but any sweet, firm apple will work), peeled, cored, and cubed
3 tbsp sugar
about 1 cup (200 g) fresh or frozen blackberries

FOR THE CRUMBLE TOPPING
1¼ cups (150 g) all-purpose flour
pinch of salt
1 tsp cinnamon
7 tbsp (100 g) cold butter, cut into chunks
1¼ cups (100 g) muesli or oatmeal
½ cup (100 g) packed light brown sugar

Preheat the oven to 350°F (180°C). Butter a 5-cup (1-l) baking dish.

Put the apples, 1 tbsp water, and the sugar in a medium saucepan and bring to a boil, stirring. Lower the heat and let the apples simmer until they're pulp.

Let the apple pulp cool. Spoon half into the prepared baking dish. Sprinkle with half of the blackberries. Repeat this step with the rest of the fruit.

Make the crumble topping: Sift the flour with the salt and cinnamon into a large bowl. Cut in the butter with your fingertips until the mixture resembles coarse bread crumbs.

Stir in the muesli and brown sugar.

Sprinkle this mixture over the fruit in the baking dish and bake the crumble about 35 minutes, until it is golden brown and juice bubbles up along the edges.

Serve the crumble immediately, so it's nicely hot, with custard or with the cardamom ice cream on page 208.

WHITE CHOCOLATE & STAR ANISE MOUSSE

⇒⇒⟶ FOR A BIG
BOWL &
MANY LITTLE ⟵⟵⟵
SPOONS

LET 6 STAR ANISE STEEP
IN 3/4 CUP + 1 TBSP (200 ML)
HEAVY CREAM OVER
LOW HEAT.

TURN OFF THE HEAT
& STIR 9 OZ (250 G)
CHOPPED WHITE
CHOCOLATE INTO
THE HOT CREAM

LET IT MELT, THEN
STRAIN INTO A LARGE
SERVING BOWL.

WHIP ANOTHER
3/4 CUP + 1 TBSP (200 ML)
HEAVY CREAM UNTIL
STIFF, THEN FOLD IT
GENTLY INTO THE
WHITE CHOCOLATE
MIXTURE → PUT IT
IN THE FRIDGE FOR
4 HOURS TO FIRM UP.

233

cinnamon citadel cake with chocolate ganache, ginger confit & dark rum

FOR THE CAKES

(Because this batter doubles in size
and you need to work carefully
and quickly, I suggest you make
this recipe two times! one after
the other. Make the big (the
bottom) cake first and then
the other two. This will also
probably fit better in your oven.)

4 eggs

½ cup plus 1 tbsp (120 g) packed
light brown sugar

pinch of salt

½ cup plus 2 tbsp (75 g) all-purpose
flour, sifted

3 tbsp (25 g) cornstarch, sifted

2 tbsp cinnamon

FOR THE GANACHE

18 oz (500 g) dark chocolate,
chopped

7 tbsp (100 g) butter

2 cups (500 ml) heavy cream

a few tbsp dark rum or cinnamon
liqueur (optional)

FOR GARNISH

2 jars ginger balls in syrup

½ cup plus 2 tbsp (150 ml) dark rum

silver dragees or shelled pistachios
(optional)

5 oz (150 g) marzipan, food coloring
of choice, and cutting forms, or
imagination and a sharp knife
(optional)

confectioners' sugar or
unsweetened cocoa powder to
dust over the cake

Make the cakes: Preheat the oven to 350°F (175°C). Grease a 9½- or 10½-inch (24- to 26-cm) springform pan and two incrementally smaller ones with butter(the three cakes will pile up into a graduated stack). Line the bottoms with parchment paper and butter these too.

With a hand mixer, beat the eggs with the sugar and salt until very stiff. It should turn almost white and triple in volume. This will take a while, so be patient.

In small batches, add the flour, cornstarch, and cinnamon, using a spatula to carefully fold it through the batter, keeping it airy and light.

Pour the batter into the pans. Put them in the middle of the oven and bake for 30 minutes until firm to the touch and golden brown. DO NOT open the oven before 30 minutes are up. If you can still easily press the cake in the middle, leave in the oven for another 5 minutes. The cakes should be ready almost at the same time.

Leave the cakes to cool for 5 minutes in the pans and then un-mold them. Let them cool completely on a rack. The cakes will sink a little, but that's fine.

Make the ganache: Slowly melt the chocolate with the butter in a bowl set over a saucepan of simmering water.

Stir as little as possible and don't let the chocolate get too hot or it will become dull and stiff and you'll need to start over.

Let the chocolate mixture cool completely. Whip the cream in a large bowl. Fold the chocolate into the whipped cream. You can also fold in some rum or liqueur. Spoon into a pastry bag and refrigerate until use.

Split all the cakes horizontally into 2 layers with the longest knife you can find. Wipe crumbs away and clean the counter. Drizzle some ginger syrup and the dark rum over the cake bottoms.

Spread all the cake bottoms with the chocolate ganache, and also the tops of the two larger cakes. This way the cakes will stick together nicely. Reserve some of the ganache for garnish. Assemble the cake halves, then stack the cakes in decreasing size. Pipe nice blobs of ganache on the seams where the cakes meet and garnish them with ginger balls, silver dragees, pistachios, and/or marzipan shapes: It may be a bit extravagant, but that's what makes it fun.

Dust the cake with confectioners' sugar and/or cocoa powder.

235

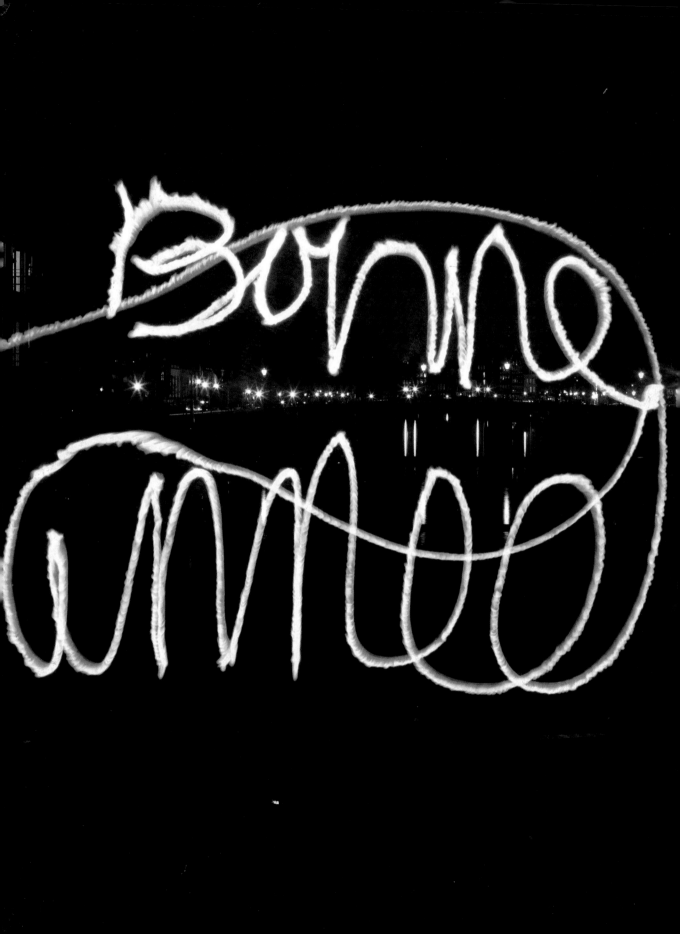

NEW YEARS EVE

DECEMBER 31, NEW YEAR'S EVE.
IT'S A BIG EVENT EVERY YEAR: WITH WHOM
WILL WE CELEBRATE? WHAT WILL WE DO? THERE'S
A NERVOUS CALLING AROUND FOR INVITATIONS
TO A GOOD PARTY . . . WHICH IS OFTEN
A DISAPPOINTMENT. PROBABLY BECAUSE
EXPECTATIONS ARE SO HIGH. THE BEST
NEW YEAR'S EVES ARE WITH YOUR BEST FRIENDS,
A GRAND DINNER THAT NEVER SEEMS TO END AND
THAT KNOCKS ON YOUR DOOR AGAIN THE NEXT DAY.
SO WE CELEBRATE JANUARY 1 WITH THOSE SAME FRIENDS.
WE WATCH MOVIES, WEAR SWEATPANTS, AND BRING OUR
BLANKETS AND PILLOWS. AND THAT DAY WE EAT
EVERYTHING. EVERYTHING WE LIKE.

oliebollen (doughnut balls)

2 cups (500 ml) lukewarm milk
1 (¼-oz / 7-g) envelope active dry
    yeast
3 tbsp sugar
4 cups (500 g) all-purpose flour
pinch of salt
1 egg
filling of choice (optional, below)

2 quarts (2 l) vegetable oil for frying
confectioners' sugar

Combine the lukewarm milk with the yeast and the sugar in a small bowl. Let stand for 10 minutes. In a large bowl, sift the flour with the salt. Make a depression in the middle and crack the egg into it. Add the yeast mixture and beat with a hand mixer, adding more milk if needed to make a thick batter, like a cake batter.

If you wish, add a filling to the batter.

Cover the batter and set aside in a warm place to rise.

Heat the oil in a large saute pan or deep-fry pan to 350°F (180°C).

With a wet ice-cream scoop or 2 greased spoons, make balls of batter and let them slide into the hot oil. Depending on their size, you can fry 4 to 8 at a time. Flip them after a few minutes. Depending on their size, they should fry for about 6 minutes, until golden. Drain on paper towels.

Serve sprinkled with powdered sugar.

cranberry balls with white chocolate

¾ cup (125 g) dried cranberries,
    soaked in warm rum or water or
    tea and drained
4½ oz (125 g) white chocolate, in
    small chunks

Stir the filling into the batter and continue as described above.

apricot rounds with almond

4½ oz (125 g) dried apricots, cut into
    small chunks, soaked in warm
    rum or water or tea and drained
⅔ cup (100 g) sliced almonds
½ tbsp almond extract (find a
    good one)

Stir the filling into the batter and continue as described above.

banana beignets with coconut

⅔ cup (100 g) shredded coconut
3 or 4 bananas, halved and halved
    again lengthwise (for 4 pieces)

Stir the coconut into the batter at the filling stage. Let the batter rise. Dip the banana pieces in the batter, then fry the batter-coated bananas in the hot oil, as above.

recipe index

general index

Jardin des Plantes, Paris

La grande Mosquée, Paris

SORTIE
→

SORTIE
←

DANK
THANK YOU,
ET MERCI:

OOF ♡

JORIS, HERO OF HEROES &
ALL THE AAN DE AMSTELS

MY SISTER SOPHIE & GUUSJE FOR HELP,
ADVICE, AND COMPANY (DAY AND NIGHT)

JOANNA & EVERYONE IN IRELAND FOR YOUR KIND RECIPES.

VICTOR, MARIETTE & RENSKE FOR TAKING THE PICTURES
WITHOUT KNOWING I WOULD USE THEM.

LA FAMILLE COLOMBET, POUR L'AMINTIÉ & VOS RECETTES.

LIESKE & MARIETTE: COOL MOTHERS EXIST. HURRAY! QUASH.